PASTA sfoglia

PASTA sfoglia

FROM OUR TABLE TO YOURS, MORE THAN 100 FRESH, SEASONAL PASTA DISHES

RON AND COLLEEN SUHANOSKY

with Susan Simon

WILEY

JOHN WILEY & SONS, INC.

For general information on our other products and services or for technical support, please contact our Customer Care Department within the United States at (800) 762-2974, outside the United States at (317) 572-3993 or fax (317) 572-4002.

Wiley also publishes its books in a variety of electronic formats. Some content that appears in print may not be available in electronic books. For more information about Wiley products, visit our Web site at www.wiley.com.

Design by Vertigo Design NYC

Library of Congress Cataloging-in-Publication Data:
Suhanosky, Ron.
  Pasta Sfoglia / Ron & Colleen Suhanosky, with Susan Simon.
     p. cm.
  Includes index.
  ISBN 978-0-470-37133-6 (cloth)
  1. Cookery (Pasta) 2. Cookery, Italian. 3. Sfoglia (Restaurant) I. Suhanosky, Colleen. II. Simon, Susan, 1945- III. Title.
  TX809.M17S92 2009
  641.8'22--dc22
                              2009019339

Printed in China

10 9 8 7 6 5 4 3 2 1

For my grandmother, Rachel Gaudino, and
for Colleen's grandfather, Joseph Piazza, whose
sense of style, sophistication, ambition,
and dedication to tradition
has influenced our lives in every way

acknowledgments

THE FIRST THING I THINK ABOUT when I wake up in the morning is pasta. As I remember all the great people who have influenced, inspired, and supported my passion for pasta and, therefore, this book, I've chosen to show my appreciation with a plate of my favorite *primo piatto* made especially for them.

My biggest thank you goes to my wife, Colleen. Colleen, my partner and dedicated mother of our three children, has a special way of thinking about food that continues to inspire me. The first pasta that I made for Colleen was spaghetti tossed with a raw tomato sauce. With deep gratitude and affection, I give her *un grande piatto di spaghetti con salsa cruda*.

My first cooking job was for my great-grandma Big Nonna, Rose Carbone. Every Sunday she would shout to me from her kitchen, "Testing time!" I would taste the pasta cooking on her stove for doneness, and she would then serve it with her special Chicken Ragù. Big Nonna, for you, my interpretation of your recipe.

Both of my grandmothers showed me the importance of all the family being together around the table. Thank you to my grandmother Rachel Gaudino, who shared her recipe for Holiday Crab and Lobster Sauce; I share my version with her. To my Polish/Hungarian grandmother, Irene Suhanosky—Grandma 'Nosky—whose use of ingredients has influenced my cooking style in many ways, I give my Whole Wheat Spaghetti, Cabbage, Wild Mushrooms, Guanciale, Caraway.

To my mother and father, Valerie and Ronald, who worked hard to ensure that my dreams could be realized, and who patiently tasted my first attempts at gnocchi making, although they referred to them as "sinkers," I serve a big bowl of my greatly improved gnocchi tossed with their favorite Bolognese sauce.

Inheriting history from the famous Café di Napoli in Minneapolis, which Colleen's grandfather Joseph Piazza opened in the 1940s, has helped us create a special setting in both Sfoglia restaurants. For my mentor in the restaurant business, Joe Piazza, I carry on his tradition of classic lasagne.

For Colleen's mother and father, Carol and John Marnell, for sharing their love of growing vegetables and showing us the importance of the earth, I bring their family tradition of cannelloni to the table.

I want to give a *mille grazie* to Susan Simon for her advice, guidance, and yes, criticism—all of which have helped me further define and articulate my passion for food. Susan's enthusiasm for food and words has been invaluable in the shaping and construction of this book. I think Susan would be very pleased with a plate of my Gnocchi, Chicken Livers, Hazelnuts, Raisins, Vin Santo.

I would like to give many thanks to all the great people I have met along the way who have been particularly kind to me and Colleen. Chefs, authors, and teachers who have been generous with their insights and advice: Michelle Scicolone, David Burke, Lidia Shire, Susan Regis, Rita D'Angelo, Marisa Iocco, Danilo LaRusso, Nonna LaRusso, Benedetta Valdi, Fabio Picchi, Lorenzo and Eileen DeMonaco, Donna Leonard, Alberto Avalle, Marida Cuccuracci, and Nancy Verde Barr.

Steadfast friends whose goodwill has gone beyond the usual: Bryan and Kathy Marsal, Louis Ceruzzi, Laura Simon and Jimmy Gross, Ray Owen, Bob and Ellen Grimes, Louise Fili, and John Derian.

The dedicated people who have helped bring Sfoglia to the table: Molly Smith, my first New York chef de cuisine; Nathan Smith; Jennifer Nelson; Adrien Martin; Alison Fosgren and Willy LeMay; Alice Fiddian-Green; Malcolm Brooks; and Jordi Cabre. Balmoris "Bobby" Mendoza, my man on Nantucket, who makes it possible for me to have two businesses on two different islands at the same time.

Our "Auntie," Celia Santos, for taking such good care of our kids, Vivian, Marcella, and Roman.

For the belief that Sfoglia could be published in the form of a cookbook, I give thanks to my agent, Susan Ginsburg, and to the people at John Wiley & Sons for being good shepherds of this project. Photographer Ben Fink, for his great photos of my food and family. Roy Finamore's keen eye is evident in the way he styled the photos. To Alison Lew at Vertigo Design, for understanding and expressing what Sfoglia is about through the design of this book.

I wouldn't have a reason to cook if it weren't for all the regular diners at both Sfoglia restaurants, Nantucket and New York City. I want to thank them for their continuous support. *Mille grazie e buon appetito!*

FROM SUSAN SIMON: I knew that something special was going on the first time I had a bowl of pasta at the original Sfoglia restaurant on Nantucket. As I continued to frequent Ron and Colleen's charming restaurant and eat their delicious food, a friendship developed. It was a friendship rooted in our mutual passion for all things Italian. When the Suhanoskys opened their New York City Sfoglia just several subway stops away from me, our relationship expanded. Actually, it grew into this cookbook. I want to thank Ron and Colleen for giving me the opportunity to share the experience of *Pasta Sfoglia* with them. *Grazie mille!*

contents

introduction

EVERY SUNDAY OF MY CHILDHOOD my family had a big meal in the middle of the day at my great-grandmother's home. At just the right moment, Big Nonna (as she was known, to differentiate her from my grandmother, Nonna) would call me over to the stove. I was her official helper. Specifically, my job was to test the pasta. I'd take a strand of spaghetti or linguine out of the boiling water and throw it against the sink's backsplash: If it stuck, it was ready. The pasta would then be served with one of our family's favorite sauces, which could include a spicy tomato sauce filled with crabs and lobster that had been cooked for an entire day in order to squeeze every last drop of flavor from the seafood—or a meat ragù made with pork meatballs and sweet Italian sausages that had been simmering on the stove top for at least twenty-four hours.

From those childhood days, pasta became my passion. I think about it all the time. When my wife, Colleen, and I met, we were happy to discover that we shared an Italian heritage, and for both of us that ancestry came from our mothers' families. Almost immediately, our conversations centered around the Italian food of our childhoods, bringing us closer together and inspiring us to travel to Italy together. In Italy, we began to refine our thinking about food.

Before we left on our trip, we were able, through some American friends, to set up a cooking apprenticeship at La Crota Ristorante in the Piedmontese town of Roddi, just outside the truffle capital of Italy, Alba. Magically, once we got there, one job led to another, and we wound up staying in Italy for nearly a year as we went on to work in Reggio Emilia at Ristorante Picci, and in Florence at the renowned Cibrèo restaurant.

At La Crota, we were immediately thrust into the truffle season. After a few miscommunications with Danilo LaRusso, the owner of the restaurant, we

were finally picked up at the train station in Alba. He looked at us, then at our suitcases. "American?" he asked. "Yes," we replied. He piled us into his old Fiat and brought us directly to the restaurant. Plates of food began to arrive: *carne crudo* covered with shaved white truffles. *Tajarin*, dialect for tagliatelle, tossed with butter, then covered with shaved white truffles. Steaming, fragrant, savory braised meat, again covered in shaved white truffles. We were easily won over.

The next day we went to work. Every morning I stood beside Danilo's mother making pasta. I learned how to make those delicious tajarin that were part of our first meal at the restaurant, and I learned to make the signature Piedmontese filled pasta called *agnolotti*. Colleen immediately immersed herself in baked goods, sweet and savory.

When our stay at La Crota ended, Danilo treated us to a few days' vacation at a friend's hotel in Liguria on the Riviera, where the discovery of new dishes from *la cucina ligure* surprised and delighted us. Then we began our next apprenticeship at Ristorante Picci. We arrived in Reggio Emilia at the end of November, when the weather seemed to be permanently gray and rainy. We were homesick and wanted to celebrate Thanksgiving with our families. However, we quickly established a good working relationship with the Picci family. Located in Italy's agricultural heartland—the majority of Italy's wheat for flour is grown in the region, and there is a large dairy industry as well—their restaurant served such traditional food as *pappardelle alla Bolognese*, *tortellini in brodo*, and *gnocco fritto*, fried dough served with prosciutto, which we made daily.

In addition to running the restaurant, the Picci family made balsamic vinegar, one of the most famous products of the region. As we learned about the lengthy vinegar-producing process, we also began to discover the many and varied uses for the aged, nectarlike product. I remember a stunning dish of shredded radicchio sautéed with balsamic vinegar then stuffed into ravioli, which were garnished with crumbled amaretti cookies and brown butter. Colleen still makes a snack for our children that we were first served during our time with the Picci family—a dish of sliced pears with chunks of Parmesan cheese doused with drops of syrupy, super-aged balsamic vinegar.

Emilia-Romagna is widely considered to be the fresh and filled pasta capital of Italy. During our free time we took trips into the nearby capital city of the region, Reggio Emilia, where we were impressed by the number of shops devoted to making fresh pasta. We enjoyed watching the *sfogline*, women pasta makers, as their hands and fingers ably formed tortellini filled with potatoes and cabbage; cappellacci filled with squash; pappardelle; tagliatelle; tagliarini; and wide sheets of lasagna noodles.

After we left Ristorante Picci, we traveled around northern Europe for a few weeks, making stops in Germany, Austria, and Denmark. However, having learned that Cibrèo restaurant in Florence often accepted apprentices in their kitchen, we were soon on a train again, this time heading south. The Cibrèo experience was the most stimulating of our working time in Italy. We were in the center of one of the world's great historic cities and we were working in the kitchen of the dynamic chef Fabio Picchi. Fabio was a real eccentric and a truly charming man with shoulder-length gray hair and a goatee that reached down to mid-chest. The food that came out of his kitchen was classic in every sense of the restaurant's name—*il cibrèo* is a traditional Florentine dish made with chicken livers, wattles, cockscombs, and other leftover chicken parts. In addition to *il cibrèo*, there was an exceptional chicken liver pâté smeared on crostini; *colli di pollo ripieni*, chicken necks stuffed with chicken forcemeat and then poached; and *farinata*, a Tuscan cabbage soup thickened with cornmeal. From Fabio, we learned to utilize every part of every ingredient that was used in his kitchen, whether it was animal or vegetable.

Filled with the wisdom and techniques we had acquired from our Italian apprenticeship, we returned to the States and worked for a couple of years as chefs at several Boston restaurants. As valuable as those experiences were, we became restless again and wanted new ones. That led us to New York City, where Colleen joined the great pastry chef Claudia Fleming at Gramercy Tavern, and I soon found a job as the chef at Il Buco, a restaurant at the edge of the East Village. After a few months, Il Buco's owners offered me a summer position working at a friend's *agriturismo*—a farm, sanctioned by the Italian government, that offers tourists room and board. We set off for Il Poggio dei Petti Rossi. The Hill of the Robin Redbreasts is located in the medieval Umbrian hillside town of Bevagna, just across a valley and within clear sight of the world-famous town Assisi. As the chef at Il Poggio, my job was to discover, and learn about, the significant dishes of that part of Umbria. It was also my responsibility to stay true to the philosophy behind the *agriturismo*, which is to use only products that are grown on the property or that come from nearby producers.

Umbria is known all over Italy for the abundance and quality of its legumes—lentils, chick peas, and an ugly-but-tasty bean called *cicerchia*. We often took advantage of this bounty in such dishes as penne with lentils and rigatoni with chick peas. We also served fish and meat, simply prepared *alle braccie*—grilled over a wood fire—and roasted potatoes in the embers. We stuffed every vegetable that we could with whatever was available—sausages, fresh herbs, nuts, and bread crumbs—then roasted them to accentuate the flavors. During our time in Bevagna, Colleen and I felt more connected to the earth and its ingredients than we did at any other time during our culinary journey.

When Colleen and I began to integrate those experiences with the Sundays in my great-grandmother's kitchen, and her family's long history in the food business, which included her grandfather Joe Piazza's landmark Minneapolis restaurant Café di Napoli, we felt confident enough to finally focus on opening our own restaurant. Our many travels and experiences, both stateside and abroad, gave me the opportunity to define an idea that I had had for years.

Serendipitously, while we were searching the real-estate listings for restaurant spaces, a place for rent on Nantucket practically popped off the page. We had been married on the island just the year before, so somehow it seemed as though fate was intervening when shortly thereafter we went to Nantucket to look at the space and to celebrate our first anniversary. Our decision was easy. We pulled up to the door and instantly knew we had found the home of our restaurant.

This was the place that would enable us to bring our ideas about food, ambience, and service literally to the table. This was the place where my grandmother's porcelain-topped kitchen tables and trusted pieces of equipment from Colleen's grandfather's Café di Napoli would live together. Just as these furnishings from our family histories would turn our restaurant into a comfortable setting, the food that would come out of our kitchen would reflect the personal story of our lives.

Since I've been driven by a love for pasta for as long as I can remember—years ago, when I saw the word *sfoglia*—meaning an uncut sheet of pasta—written down in a book of Italian gastronomy, I was seduced and I knew from that moment that it would be the name of a future restaurant. Now, with our restaurant named, we were ready to go.

In some ways, the pace of life on Nantucket was similar to what we had experienced in the small Italian towns where we had worked. On the island, we were able to practice our cooking style at the same speed we had become accustomed to while in Italy. We easily met island farmers and fishermen who introduced us to the local resources that we needed to integrate what we had learned about cooking from our families, work, and travel experiences. In Sfoglia's kitchen, we continued to apply our knowledge not just of specific Italian dishes, but also of the Italian way of cooking. We had learned that sauces don't necessarily need to cook for hours and hours, as they had on my great-grandmother's stove, in order to achieve depth of flavor. The flavor can also come from fresh ingredients, grown and raised nearby, and the simplicity of their preparation. We learned that when you pair sweet and savory in the same dish, you can create startling new flavors, simply and quickly. This way of presenting food is straight out of the Italian Renaissance kitchen.

Some of the dishes that I've created using the collected themes of past experiences, local ingredients, and the sweet and savory combination of flavors that define the Renaissance kitchen are Spaghetti, Strawberries, Tomato, Balsamic (page 68); Gnocchi, Chicken Livers, Hazelnuts, Raisins, Vin Santo (page 142); and Risotto all'Amarone, Prunes, Crushed Amaretti (page 181). These dishes are part of the foundation of Sfoglia's cooking style.

As our restaurant on Nantucket grew, so did our family. Our daughters, Vivian and Marcella, were born on Nantucket three years apart. When we began to think about the future, we realized that our family needed bigger challenges and more opportunities. So, once again we made a trip south down I-95 to New York City. We knew the city well from our past experiences and its spirit had always been with us.

Without abandoning our island Sfoglia, six years after its birth we opened a second Sfoglia on Manhattan's Upper East Side. A year later our son, Roman, was born. Our family was complete.

We considered ourselves fortunate that as soon as we had opened the new restaurant's doors, we were immediately successful and received enthusiastic critical notice. Just about every reviewer singled out our pasta dishes as outstanding menu attractions. So when we thought about writing a cookbook, only one subject came to mind—pasta. I consider pasta to be anything that's made with a grain. Therefore, you will find recipes for fresh pasta, dry pasta, and filled pasta, as well as for gnocchi, risotto, farro, and polenta.

As you make your way through this book, you will learn more about how our experiences inspired our recipes. You'll find that as you take this journey, there are certain methods that are repeated throughout the recipes. Some are methods that I learned, such as adding pasta water to sauces to help the sauce adhere to the pasta, not absorb it. From Alberto, one of the owners of Il Buco, I learned to cut all the ingredients that go into a sauce the same size as the pasta so that everything can be easily picked up in the same forkful. And from Nonna LaRusso at La Crota Ristorante, I learned that when you make pasta dough with duck eggs, not only is its color enriched, but its texture is silkier than when it's made with the more traditional chicken eggs.

Other methods are ones that I've devised through many trials with both ingredients and equipment. For example, I use grape seed oil to start just about all of my recipes. It's my fat of choice because its neutral flavor doesn't interfere with the other ingredients that are meant to be the stars of the dish. I use water instead of protein-based broths as the liquid for making risottos. Chicken or meat broths tend to break down the rice kernels, resulting in a mushy dish. Perhaps the most important contribution I've made is a way to make sophisticated pasta dishes with efficiency and ease: by combining ingredients that offer flavors from salty to sweet with tart in between; and textures that can be achieved with creamy sauces, crunchy ingredients like roasted nuts, and the pasta itself.

Colleen and I hope that when you begin to cook with these simple but unusual, out-of-the-ordinary recipes, you will make the best pasta that you've ever tasted and be inspired to bring your own traditions to your table.

pantry

THIS SECTION INCLUDES NOT ONLY INGREDIENTS THAT I TEND TO USE OVER AND OVER AGAIN, BUT ALSO A FEW THAT ARE WORTH HAVING AROUND BECAUSE OF THEIR LONG SHELF LIVES. THE RESOURCES LIST ON PAGE 194 WILL GUIDE YOU TO SHOPPING SITES THAT CARRY EVERYTHING INCLUDED HERE.

GRAPE SEED OIL Although this oil is slightly more expensive than others, I feel it's worth spending the extra money because of its diversity of use and its neutral flavor, which lets whatever is cooked in it be the starring ingredient. Its high flash point allows for searing at intensely high heat. You can also use much less of it than you do with other oils because it expands when it's heated.

EXTRA VIRGIN OLIVE OIL I like to use extra virgin olive oil with raw sauces like the various herb and nut pestos, and to finish sauces. I prefer Sicilian extra virgin olive oil because I like what its fruity flavor brings to my dishes. I find the northern oils, in particular Tuscan oils, too peppery tasting for my style of cooking. However, there are a few recipes that call for olive oil in cooked sauces. For these dishes I use pure olive oil.

KOSHER SALT I'm partial to kosher salt because its triangular crystals adhere evenly to the food to which it's added, allowing for true seasoning.

BLACK PEPPERCORNS In Italy, freshly cracked black pepper is used primarily as a rub when curing meats, specifically pork products like guanciale and dry sausages. Italians prefer to spice their food with *peperoncini*, hot red pepper flakes. They view black pepper as too fragrant—perfumelike—and as something that muddies the flavor of food to which it's added. However, I use black pepper in just about every dish in this book. Adding cracked black pepper in moderation heightens the flavors of the other ingredients in a dish.

CANNED SAN MARZANO TOMATOES When I call for pureed tomatoes in a recipe, I like to start out with San Marzano whole tomatoes because the flavor of a whole tomato is more concentrated than that of a tomato that has been pureed before it was canned. The thick flesh of the San Marzano variety of plum tomatoes makes a good, thick puree. Although San Marzano tomatoes can be grown anywhere, real ones will have a DOC (Denominazione di Origine Controllata) symbol on the can, assuring you that the tomato was ripened on the vine before it was processed and canned, and that it was grown in or near the town of San Marzano, in the Campania region, where Naples is the capital.

FLOUR I have a short list of flours that I keep on hand to make fresh pasta or gnocchi. *Doppio zero*, 00 flour, is an Italian finely milled white flour. I also keep smaller supplies of whole wheat, buckwheat, and farro flour to use specifically for fresh pasta.

RICE FLOUR This flour holds less moisture than any other flour. It's perfect for dusting fresh pasta and gnocchi while you're making them: It keeps your hands dry while you work with the dough and grabs onto wetter flours, making them easier to handle. I dust rice flour onto freshly made pasta and gnocchi when I want to store them for a few hours. I also use rice flour in my cavatelli dough because it lightens it, thereby making it easier to feed through the cavatelli maker.

CARNAROLI RICE This short-grained rice is my first choice for risotto because it evenly releases its starch when liquid is added to it, making for a perfect, creamy dish.

RISO VENERE This rice, of Chinese origin, was once considered to be the "rice of the emperors," and only the nobility could eat it. It is now grown in the southern part of the Lombardy and Piedmont provinces in Italy. I like its strong, nutty flavor and its beautiful, shiny black color. There's a wonderful contrast of taste and appearance when it's made into a dish.

FARRO Farro is an ancient wheatlike grain that's often called emmer in English. Farro is often mistakenly referred to as spelt. It's not. While the grains look alike, they cook differently. Emmer cooks faster than spelt. Unlike rice, farro doesn't release starch as it cooks. Instead, it absorbs the liquid it's cooked in. I use the whole grain and the *speziato*, or cracked, in my recipes.

NUTS For flavor and texture, I use walnuts, almonds, pistachios, hazelnuts, and pine nuts in many of my recipes. I always toast the nuts before I add them to a dish, to bring out their natural oils and intensify their flavor.

DRIED FRUITS I use raisins (black and golden), currants, and prunes because of their intense flavor and their ability to keep their shape, especially in a braised sauce. Most of all, they provide sweetness for the sweet and savory combinations of flavors that I like.

SAFFRON There is a great tradition of saffron as an ingredient in the Italian kitchen. Perhaps the most well-known use is in turning *risotto alla Milanese* golden. In Italy, saffron grows in the Abruzzo region, where it is a seasoning in many seafood dishes. I use saffron to flavor pasta sauces and risotto toppings.

PEPERONCINI—HOT RED PEPPER FLAKES You could say that peperoncini are the most personal of all Italian spices. Many households keep a hot red pepper plant growing all year round in their backyards, on balconies, or on windowsills. This way the plants can serve the dual purpose of being at the ready when needed to flavor food—and, according to popular belief, to ward off evil spirits.

AMARETTI COOKIES These commercially manufactured cookies are made simply with crushed bitter almonds, egg whites, and sugar. Widely used, especially in northern Italy, amaretti are a versatile ingredient in pastas, vegetables, and poultry fillings, as well as in desserts and as a garnish. They add what I think of as an immature sweetness, or semisweet flavor, and a nice crunch.

PARMESAN CHEESE Parmesan cheese is an essential ingredient in recipes such as cream sauces, pesto, risotto, and polenta. It's also an optional garnish for most tomato sauces. I prefer to use real Parmigiano Reggiano because of its nutty flavor and almost crystalline texture.

master RECIPES

These recipes are the fondamenta—*the foundation—
around which all my other recipes are structured. Just
like a foundation is built with strong, immovable stone,
these recipes are set in stone and need to be precisely
followed in order for all the other recipes to be easy.*

fresh egg PASTA

SITTING AT THE TABLE IN MY GREAT-GRANDMOTHER'S KITCHEN, WATCHING HER MAKE PASTA, IS WHERE MY STORY BEGINS. AT HER HOME EVERY SUNDAY, INSTEAD OF PLAYING WITH MY SISTERS, I GRAVITATED TOWARD THE KITCHEN, FOND OF THE COMFORT I FELT BEING AROUND BIG NONNA—MY MOTHER'S GRANDMOTHER. I LIKED THE WAY SHE MOVED AROUND HER KITCHEN.

I WATCHED HER MAKE MANY PASTA DISHES, AND FOR THOSE THAT REQUIRED FRESH PASTA, I WATCHED HER MAKE THAT, TOO. I BOUGHT MY FIRST HAND-CRANK PASTA MAKER WHEN I WAS SIXTEEN, AND IT WASN'T LONG BEFORE I STARTED TO EXPERIMENT WITH MAKING MY OWN VERSIONS OF HER EGG PASTA. OVER THE YEARS, I HAVE REFINED MY DOUGH RECIPE UNTIL I FINALLY SETTLED ON THIS ONE. I'VE ALSO REALIZED THAT AN ELECTRIC MACHINE IS THE MOST EXPEDITIOUS WAY TO ROLL AND CUT PASTA. BECAUSE THE ELECTRIC MACHINE WORKS SO QUICKLY AND PRECISELY, THE TASK OF MAKING FRESH PASTA BECOMES LESS INTIMIDATING.

I FIND THAT THE FOOD PROCESSOR METHOD WORKS BEST WHEN YOU'RE MAKING A SMALL AMOUNT OF DOUGH. THE BLADE OF THE PROCESSOR NOT ONLY INCORPORATES THE INGREDIENTS, BUT ALSO HELPS TO KNEAD THE DOUGH.

MAKES ABOUT 1 POUND DOUGH | SERVES 4–6

| 2 cups all-purpose flour | 2 teaspoons extra virgin olive oil | Rice flour for dusting |
| 3 eggs | 1 teaspoon kosher salt | |

1. Add the all-purpose flour, eggs, extra virgin olive oil, and salt to the bowl of a food processor fitted with a metal blade. Pulse several times until the dough resembles medium crumbs.

2. Turn out the dough onto a clean, dry, rice flour–dusted work surface. Gather the dough together and knead it until it comes together and is smooth and elastic. Cover the dough with a kitchen towel or plastic film and let rest for at least 10 minutes or up to 2 hours.

STORAGE: *The dough, tightly wrapped with plastic film, can be refrigerated for up to 2 days or frozen for up to 2 weeks. Defrost in the refrigerator. The dough will discolor slightly, but its flavor will not be affected.*

THIS DOUGH IS USED FOR: *pappardelle, tagliatelle, fettuccine, lasagne, rotoli, spaghetti, and filled pasta.*

sfoglia's duck egg PASTA

COLLEEN AND I SPENT A TRUFFLE SEASON, SEPTEMBER THROUGH NOVEMBER, AT LA CROTA RISTORANTE IN ALBA. THERE, NONNA LARUSSO, THE OWNER'S MOTHER, TAUGHT ME THE SECRET FOR GIVING FRESH EGG PASTA A RICHER COLOR—SHE ADDED EGG YOLKS. THIS WAS HER TYPICAL PRACTICE WHEN MAKING THE TAGLIATELLE TO SERVE *AL TARTUFO*, WITH FRESH TRUFFLES. SOMETIMES, HOWEVER, SHE USED DUCK EGGS FOR THE SAME REASON—DEEPER COLOR AND ALSO TO GIVE THE DOUGH A MORE SATINY FEEL. I STORED THE IDEA IN THE BACK OF MY MIND, ALONG WITH THE OTHER TECHNIQUES THAT I DISCOVERED IN ITALY.

LATER, WHEN WE OPENED OUR FIRST SFOGLIA RESTAURANT ON NANTUCKET, WE TRIED TO RESOURCE DUCK EGGS TO USE IN *OUR* PASTA. ALTHOUGH WE FOUND AN ISLANDER WHO WOULD TRADE HER DUCK EGGS FOR SFOGLIA BREAD, THERE JUST WEREN'T ENOUGH EGGS FOR OUR NEEDS. EVENTUALLY, WE FOUND A COMMERCIAL SUPPLIER (SEE RESOURCES, PAGE 194).

THE DOPPIO ZERO (00) FLOUR IS WHAT IS USED IN ITALY. IT'S A FINER-MILLED FLOUR, AND THEREFORE HOLDS LESS MOISTURE (SEE RESOURCES, PAGE 194).

MAKES ABOUT 1 POUND DOUGH | SERVES 4–6

2 cups doppio zero (00) flour	2 teaspoons extra virgin olive oil	Rice flour for dusting
3 duck eggs	1 teaspoon kosher salt	

1. Add the 00 flour, eggs, extra virgin olive oil, and salt to the bowl of a food processor fitted with a metal blade. Pulse several times until the dough resembles medium crumbs.

2. Turn out the dough onto a clean, dry, rice flour–dusted work surface. Gather the dough and knead it for a few minutes until it comes together and a smooth, elastic dough is achieved. Cover the dough with a kitchen towel or plastic film and let rest for at least 10 minutes or up to 2 hours.

STORAGE: *The dough, tightly wrapped with plastic film, can be refrigerated for up to 2 days or frozen for up to 2 weeks. Defrost in the refrigerator. The dough will discolor slightly, but its flavor will not be affected.*

THIS DOUGH IS USED FOR: *pappardelle, tagliatelle, fettuccine, lasagne, rotoli, spaghetti, and filled pasta.*

whole wheat PASTA

ONCE I PERFECTED MY FRESH EGG DOUGH MADE WITH WHITE FLOUR, I BEGAN TO EXPERIMENT WITH MAKING THE DOUGH WITH WHOLE WHEAT FLOUR. I QUICKLY DISCOVERED THAT IN ORDER TO MAKE THE DOUGH ELASTIC ENOUGH TO ROLL OUT, IT NEEDED A HIGHER GLUTEN CONTENT THAN WHOLE GRAIN FLOURS PROVIDE. ALL THE WHOLE GRAIN DOUGHS INCLUDE THE ADDITION OF ALL-PURPOSE FLOUR.

I ALSO NOTICED THAT THERE WERE DIFFERENT SAUCES THAT WORKED PARTICULARLY WELL WITH WHOLE WHEAT PASTA. THESE SAUCES TEND TO BE MORE VEGETABLE BASED, RATHER THAN PROTEIN BASED LIKE THE ONES THAT ARE OFTEN USED WITH WHITE FLOUR PASTAS. COOL- AND COLD-WEATHER VEGETABLES LIKE ARTICHOKES, KALE, MUSHROOMS, HARD-SKINNED SQUASH, AND ROOT VEGETABLES SEEM TO MAKE THE BEST MARRIAGE WITH THE CHEWY WHOLE WHEAT PASTA.

MAKES ABOUT 1 POUND DOUGH | SERVES 4–6

1⅓ cups all-purpose flour	3 eggs	1 teaspoon kosher salt
⅔ cup whole wheat flour	2 teaspoons extra virgin olive oil	Rice flour for dusting

1. Add the all-purpose flour, whole wheat flour, eggs, extra virgin olive oil, and salt to the bowl of a food processor fitted with a metal blade. Pulse several times until the dough resembles medium crumbs.

2. Turn out the dough onto a clean, dry, rice flour–dusted work surface. Gather the dough and knead it until it comes together and a smooth, elastic dough is achieved. Cover the dough with a kitchen towel or plastic film and let rest for at least 10 minutes or up to 2 hours.

STORAGE: *The dough, tightly wrapped with plastic film, can be refrigerated for up to 2 days or frozen for up to 2 weeks. Defrost in the refrigerator. The dough will discolor slightly, but its flavor will not be affected.*

THIS DOUGH IS USED FOR: *spaghetti, pappardelle, fettuccine, and tagliatelle.*

buckwheat PASTA

BUCKWHEAT PASTA DISHES ARE FOUND THROUGHOUT NORTHERN ITALY, WHERE BUCKWHEAT GROWS IN THE COOLER MOUNTAIN CLIMATE. ON ITS OWN, BUCKWHEAT PASTA HAS A STRONG AND UNIQUE FLAVOR. IT NEEDS TO BE PAIRED WITH A SAUCE THAT ENHANCES ITS BOLD FLAVOR. SAUCES THAT ARE FATTY AND INCLUDE BUTTER, CHEESE, AND CREAM WORK WELL. SO DO SAUCES THAT HAVE THEIR OWN INTENSELY FLAVORED INGREDIENTS LIKE ANCHOVIES, CAVIAR, AND CHICKEN LIVERS.

BUCKWHEAT PASTA IS REALLY AT ITS BEST WHEN USED FOR WIDER NOODLES SUCH AS PAPPARDELLE AND TAGLIATELLE. *PIZZOCCHERI* IS A BUCKWHEAT PASTA DISH FROM LOMBARDY. THE TAGLIATELLE-LIKE NOODLES (IN THIS CASE, *MALTAGLIATI*, ROUGHLY CUT PASTA) ARE COOKED IN A CABBAGE, CARROT, AND POTATO BROTH, THEN DRAINED WITH THE VEGETABLES AND TOPPED WITH A SHARP MOUNTAIN CHEESE CALLED *BITTO*.

MAKES ABOUT 1 POUND DOUGH | SERVES 4–6

1⅓ cups all-purpose flour	3 eggs	1 teaspoon kosher salt
⅔ cup buckwheat flour	2 teaspoons extra virgin olive oil	Rice flour for dusting

1. Add the all-purpose flour, buckwheat flour, eggs, extra virgin olive oil, and salt to the bowl of a food processor fitted with a metal blade. Pulse several times until the dough resembles medium crumbs.

2. Turn out the dough onto a clean, dry, rice flour–dusted work surface. Gather the dough and knead it until it comes together and a smooth, elastic dough is achieved. Cover the dough with a kitchen towel or plastic film and let rest for at least 10 minutes or up to 2 hours.

STORAGE: *The dough, tightly wrapped with plastic film, can be refrigerated for up to 2 days or frozen for up to 2 weeks. Defrost in the refrigerator. The dough will discolor slightly, but its flavor will not be affected.*

THIS DOUGH IS USED FOR: *pappardelle and tagliatelle.*

farro PASTA

FARRO IS AN ANCIENT ROMAN GRAIN. AFTER ITS HARVEST, THE GRAIN IS SORTED INTO WHOLE BERRIES AND BROKEN ONES. SOME OF THE BROKEN ONES, *SPEZIATO*, ARE SAVED FOR SOUPS AND POLENTA-LIKE DISHES. THE REST ARE MILLED INTO FLOUR. HISTORICALLY, FARRO FLOUR WAS FIRST USED TO MAKE BREAD AND CAKES. USING IT FOR PASTA CAME LATER.

MAKES ABOUT 1 POUND DOUGH | SERVES 4–6

1⅔ cups all-purpose flour	3 eggs	1 teaspoon kosher salt
⅔ cup farro flour	2 teaspoons extra virgin olive oil	Rice flour for dusting

1. Add the all-purpose flour, farro flour, eggs, extra virgin olive oil, and salt to the bowl of a food processor fitted with a metal blade. Pulse several times until the dough resembles medium crumbs.

2. Turn out the dough onto a clean, dry, rice flour–dusted work surface. Gather the dough together and knead it until it comes together and a smooth, elastic dough is achieved. Cover the dough with a kitchen towel or plastic film and let rest for at least 10 minutes or up to 2 hours.

STORAGE: *The dough, tightly wrapped with plastic film, can be refrigerated for up to 2 days or frozen for up to 2 weeks. Defrost in the refrigerator. The dough will discolor slightly, but its flavor will not be affected.*

THIS DOUGH IS USED FOR: *spaghetti, fettuccine, pappardelle, and tagliatelle.*

HOW TO *roll and cut the pasta for various shapes*

PAPPARDELLE, TAGLIATELLE, AND FETTUCCINE with an electric pasta maker

1 Divide the dough into 3 equal pieces. Flatten each piece into a disk and dust with rice flour.

2 Set the roller of the electric pasta maker at number 1. Feed the disks, one at a time, through the roller three times. Fold each end of the dough to meet in the middle and press down on the middle to seal. Feed the open side of the dough through the roller three times. Fold the ends to meet in the middle and press down to seal.

3 Adjust the setting to number 2. Feed the open side of the dough through the roller twice.

4 Adjust the setting to number 3. Feed the dough through the roller twice. The *sfoglia* will be quite long now. Cut it in half and feed each half through the roller once more. Dust each sheet with rice flour and layer one on top of the other.

5 I like to hand cut both pappardelle and fettuccine. For either cut, layer 3 *sfoglie* at a time, placing the longest piece on the bottom. Roll up into a loose roll. For pappardelle, cut each roll into 1-inch-wide pieces. For fettuccine, cut each roll into ⅓-inch-wide pieces. Loosen the rolls and stretch out the ribbons on a baking sheet. Dust with more rice flour. If you aren't going to use the pasta right away, cover it with a slightly dampened kitchen towel to keep it from drying out. Do not refrigerate—the ribbons will stick together.

PAPPARDELLE, TAGLIATELLE, AND FETTUCCINE WITH A HAND-CRANK PASTA MAKER: *Proceed as directed for the electric pasta maker. At setting number 1, fold the dough and feed it through the roller three times. On number 2, feed the dough through three times, and on number 3, three times. On number 4, cut the pasta* sfoglia *in half and feed each piece through the roller three times. On number 5, feed each* sfoglia *through once. Cut into pappardelle, tagliatelle, or fettuccine as described for the electric pasta maker.*

SPAGHETTI with an electric pasta maker

1 Divide the dough into 6 equal pieces. Flatten each piece into a disk and dust with rice flour.

2 Set the roller of the electric pasta maker at number 1 and feed the disks, one at a time, through the roller three times. Fold each end of the dough to meet in the middle and press down on the middle to seal. Fold the open side of the dough through the roller three times. Cut each sheet of pasta in half.

3 Place a spaghetti die on the pasta machine. Feed the pasta through the spaghetti die. Dust the spaghetti die with rice flour in between each sheet of pasta. This will let the pasta pass through more easily and keep the die from clogging up.

4 Store the spaghetti on a baking sheet and sprinkle with rice flour. If you aren't going to use the pasta right away, cover it with a slightly dampened kitchen towel. Do not refrigerate—spaghetti will stick together.

SPAGHETTI WITH A HAND-CRANK PASTA MAKER: *Proceed as directed for the electric pasta maker.*

FILLED PASTA: CUSCINETTI, RAVIOLI, TRIANGOLONI, TORTELLINI, LASAGNE, CANNELLONI, AND ROTOLI with an electric pasta maker

1 Divide the dough into 3 equal pieces. Flatten each piece into a disk and dust with rice flour.

2 Set the roller of the electric pasta maker at number 1. Feed the disks, one at a time, through the roller three times. Fold each end of the dough to meet in the middle and press down on the middle to seal. Feed the open side of the dough through the roller three times. Fold the ends to meet in the middle and press down to seal.

3 Adjust the setting to number 2. Feed the open side of the dough through the roller twice.

4 Adjust the setting to number 3. Feed the dough through the roller twice. The sheet will be quite long now. Cut it in half and feed each piece through the roller once more.

5 Adjust the setting to number 4. Feed the pasta *sfoglie* through the roller twice.

6 Adjust the setting to number 5. Feed the pasta *sfoglie* through the roller twice. For tortellini, feed the pasta *sfoglie* through number 5 three times. Dust each *sfoglia* with rice flour and layer one on top of the other. If you aren't going to use the pasta *sfoglie* right away, cover them with a slightly dampened kitchen towel to keep them from drying out. Do not refrigerate—the *sfoglie* will stick together.

7 Cut the pasta *sfoglie* according to the individual recipes.

FILLED PASTA WITH A HAND-CRANK PASTA MAKER: *Proceed as directed for the electric pasta maker, except at number 5, feed the pasta* sfoglie *through three times. For tortellini, four times.*

potato GNOCCHI

ONE DAY WHILE I WAS STILL IN HIGH SCHOOL, I READ A RECIPE FOR POTATO GNOC-CHI IN A FOOD MAGAZINE AND DECIDED I WOULD TRY TO MAKE THEM FOR MY FAM-ILY FOR DINNER. THE NIGHT I SERVED THEM, WITH A SIMPLE TOMATO SAUCE, I REMEMBER THAT MY FATHER CALLED THEM SINKERS, BECAUSE THEY JUST DROPPED INTO HIS STOMACH AND STAYED THERE.

AFTER THAT EMBARRASSING MEAL, I CONTINUED TO MAKE THESE LITTLE DUMPLINGS UNTIL I FINALLY FOUND THE RIGHT FORMULA. I REALIZED THAT IN ORDER TO MAKE REALLY GOOD GNOCCHI, IT IS IMPORTANT TO FEEL THE DOUGH WITH MY HANDS. THE IDEA IS TO INCORPORATE THE FLOUR INTO THE POTATOES JUST ENOUGH SO THE RESULTING DOUGH IS LIGHT AND FLUFFY, NOT ELASTIC, AS IT WOULD BE IF IT WERE MADE IN A FOOD PROCESSOR OR STAND MIXER.

ANOTHER THING THAT IS ESSENTIAL FOR GOOD GNOCCHI IS THE TEMPERATURE OF THE POTATOES WHEN THEY ARE PASSED THROUGH A FOOD MILL. THE POTATOES SHOULD BE WARM TO THE TOUCH, NOT HOT AND NOT COLD.

THESE DELICATE GNOCCHI HAVE BECOME A SIGNATURE ON THE SFOGLIA RESTAU-RANTS' MENUS, WHERE WE CHANGE THEIR SAUCES WITH THE SEASONS.

MAKES 2 POUNDS GNOCCHI

3 pounds unpeeled Idaho potatoes	2 teaspoons kosher salt	Rice flour for dusting
1 cup all-purpose flour	1 egg	

1. Gently boil the potatoes in their jackets in a large pot of water over medium heat until a tester passes easily through the thickest part. Remove the potatoes from the pot and let cool to the touch; they shouldn't get completely cold.

2. Wrap the potatoes in a kitchen towel or cotton napkin and rub to remove the skins. Pass the potatoes through a food mill fitted with a medium-hole disk, or through a ricer, into a large mixing bowl.

3. Spread the all-purpose flour on a clean, dry work surface. Place the potatoes on top of the flour. Add the salt and egg. Use your hands to gather the ingredients together and gently knead the dough into a 10 by 8-inch log. Let rest for 2 minutes.

4. Lightly dust a clean, dry work surface with rice flour. Cut the log into 4 equal pieces. Roll each piece into a 1-inch-thick rope. Cut each rope into ½-inch-wide gnocchi. Store the gnocchi on a rice flour–covered baking sheet until ready to use. Dust with rice flour.

sweet potato GNOCCHI

AFTER I FELT COMFORTABLE WITH MY DOUGH FOR POTATO GNOCCHI, I DECIDED TO TRY MAKING THEM WITH SWEET POTATOES. JUST AS IT IS WITH POTATO GNOCCHI, IT'S IMPORTANT TO USE YOUR HANDS WHEN MAKING SWEET POTATO GNOCCHI. YOU ALSO NEED TO PAY MORE ATTENTION WHEN YOU INCORPORATE THE FLOUR BECAUSE SWEET POTATOES HOLD MORE MOISTURE THAN DO IDAHOS. IF THE DOUGH IS TOO MOIST, IT WON'T ROLL PROPERLY, MAKING IT IMPOSSIBLE TO FORM GNOCCHI.

I USE MAPLE SYRUP TO ENHANCE THE FLAVOR OF THE SWEET POTATOES. AND I CUT THESE GNOCCHI INTO SLIGHTLY LARGER DUMPLINGS THAN THE POTATO GNOCCHI IN ORDER TO GET A GOOD MOUTHFUL OF THE SWEET POTATOES.

MAKES 2½ POUNDS GNOCCHI

1½ pounds unpeeled sweet potatoes	2 cups all-purpose flour	1 teaspoon kosher salt
1½ pounds unpeeled Idaho potatoes	1 egg	Rice flour for dusting
	¼ cup maple syrup	

1. Preheat the oven to 400°F. Wrap the sweet potatoes in aluminum foil. Bake until a tester passes easily through the thickest part, about 1 hour. Let cool.

2. Gently boil the Idaho potatoes in their jackets in a large pot of water over medium heat until a tester passes easily through the thickest part. Remove the potatoes from the pot and let cool to the touch; they shouldn't get completely cold.

3. Wrap the potatoes—sweet and white—in a kitchen towel or cotton napkin and rub to remove the skins. Pass the potatoes through a food mill fitted with a medium-hole disk, or through a ricer, into a large mixing bowl.

4. Spread the all-purpose flour on a clean, dry work surface. Place the potatoes on top of the flour. Add the egg, maple syrup, and salt. Use your hands to gather the ingredients together and gently knead the dough into a 10 by 8-inch log. Let rest for 2 minutes.

5. Lightly dust a clean, dry work surface with rice flour. Cut the log into 4 equal pieces. Roll each piece into a 1-inch-thick rope. Cut each rope into ½-inch gnocchi. Store the gnocchi on a rice flour–covered baking sheet until ready to use. Dust with rice flour.

STORAGE: *The gnocchi can be frozen for up to 2 weeks. To prepare them for the freezer, place them, dusted with rice flour, in a single layer on a baking sheet and freeze. Once frozen, place them one on top of the other in an airtight container. To thaw for cooking, place the gnocchi in a single layer on a baking sheet in the refrigerator for not more than 1 hour before cooking. Cook according to the recipe directions.*

butternut squash GNOCCHI

B UTTERNUT SQUASH GNOCCHI, INSPIRED BY *GNOCCHI DI ZUCCA*, PUMPKIN GNOCCHI, A TRADITIONAL DISH FROM NORTHERN ITALY'S LOMBARDY REGION, ARE EVEN MORE TEMPERAMENTAL THAN POTATO GNOCCHI. BECAUSE BUTTERNUT SQUASH DON'T CONTAIN AS MUCH STARCH AS POTATOES, YOU'LL HAVE TO KNEAD THE DOUGH A LITTLE LONGER THAN YOU DO FOR THE POTATO GNOCCHI IN ORDER TO RELEASE THE STARCH.

MAKES ABOUT 2½ POUNDS GNOCCHI

One 2- to 2½-pound butternut squash

1½ pounds unpeeled Idaho potatoes

2 cups all-purpose flour

1 egg

2 teaspoons kosher salt

¼ teaspoon freshly ground black pepper

½ teaspoon freshly grated nutmeg

Rice flour for dusting

1. Preheat the oven to 400°F. Wrap the butternut squash in aluminum foil. Bake until a tester passes easily through the thickest part of the squash, about 1½ hours.

2. Gently boil the potatoes in their jackets in a large pot of water over medium heat until a tester passes easily through the thickest part. Remove the potatoes from the pot and let cool to the touch; they shouldn't get completely cold.

3. Wrap the potatoes in a kitchen towel or cotton napkin and rub to remove the skins. Pass the potatoes through a food mill fitted with a medium-hole disk, or through a ricer, into a large mixing bowl.

4. When the squash is cool to the touch, cut it into quarters. Remove the seeds and discard. Remove the flesh and measure 2 cups. Save the remaining squash for another use. Pass the cooked squash through the food mill directly into the mixing bowl.

5. Spread the all-purpose flour on a clean, dry work surface. Place the potatoes and butternut squash on top of the flour. Add the egg, salt, pepper, and nutmeg. Use your hands to gather the ingredients together and gently knead the dough into a 10 by 8-inch log. Let rest for 2 minutes.

6. Lightly dust a dry work surface with rice flour. Cut the log into 4 equal pieces. Roll each piece into a 1-inch-thick rope. Cut each rope into ½-inch gnocchi. Store the gnocchi on a rice flour–covered baking sheet until ready for use. Dust with rice flour.

STORAGE: *The gnocchi can be frozen for up to 2 weeks. To prepare them for the freezer, place them, dusted with rice flour, in a single layer on a baking sheet and freeze. Once frozen, place them one on top of the other in an airtight container. To thaw for cooking, place the gnocchi in a single layer on a baking sheet in the refrigerator for not more than 1 hour before cooking. Cook according to the recipe directions.*

ricotta GNOCCHI

ICOTTA GNOCCHI ARE A LIGHTER ALTERNATIVE TO THE STARCHIER POTATO GNOC-CHI. THEY ARE ALSO EASIER AND QUICKER TO MAKE. WITH THEIR ALMOST FLUFFY CONSISTENCY, THEY MELT IN YOUR MOUTH.

MAKES ABOUT 2 POUNDS GNOCCHI

1 cup all-purpose flour	1 teaspoon kosher salt	1 egg
1½ pounds whole milk ricotta cheese	¼ teaspoon freshly ground black pepper	Rice flour for dusting

1. Spread the all-purpose flour on a clean, dry work surface. Place the ricotta, salt, pepper, and egg on top of the flour. Use your hands to gather the ingredients together and gently knead the dough into a 10 by 8-inch log. Let rest for 2 minutes.

2. Lightly dust a clean, dry work surface with rice flour. Cut the log into 4 equal pieces. Roll each piece into a 1-inch-thick rope. Cut each rope into ½-inch gnocchi. Store the gnocchi on a rice flour–covered baking sheet until ready to use. Dust with rice flour.

STORAGE: *The gnocchi can be frozen for up to 2 weeks. To prepare them for the freezer, place them, dusted with rice flour, in a single layer on a baking sheet and freeze. Once frozen, place them one on top of the other in an airtight container. To thaw for cooking, place the gnocchi in a single layer on a baking sheet in the refrigerator for not more than 1 hour before cooking. Cook according to the recipe directions.*

ricotta CAVATELLI

I ATE A LOT OF CAVATELLI WHEN I WAS A KID. THEY WERE ALWAYS FRESH, EVEN THOUGH THEY WEREN'T ALWAYS MADE AT HOME. MY GRANDMOTHER'S SATURDAY SHOPPING ROUTINE FOR OUR BIG SUNDAY FAMILY LUNCH WOULD INCLUDE STOPPING FOR SOME FRESH CAVATELLI AT THE LOCAL PASTA SHOP IN THE ITALIAN NEIGHBORHOOD OF NEW HAVEN, CONNECTICUT. SINCE THEN I'VE LOVED CAVATELLI, BUT IT WASN'T UNTIL I WENT TO WORK FOR DAVID BURKE AT THE PARK AVENUE CAFÉ IN NEW YORK CITY THAT I SAW A CAVATELLI MAKER IN USE. I SOON SEARCHED OUT ONE FOR MYSELF.

MY FRESH CAVATELLI IS ALWAYS MADE WITH RICOTTA CHEESE AND FRESHLY GROUND BLACK PEPPER. IT'S POSSIBLE TO FIND DRY CAVATELLI—MADE WITH ONLY FLOUR AND WATER, LIKE MOST DRY PASTA. THE NAME OF THE PASTA, *CAVATELLI*, REFERS TO ITS SHAPE, LITTLE PLUGS, NOT NECESSARILY TO THE INGREDIENTS USED TO MAKE THEM.

MAKES ABOUT 2 POUNDS CAVATELLI

2 cups all-purpose flour	¾ pound whole milk ricotta	¼ teaspoon freshly ground pepper
¾ cup rice flour, plus more for dusting	2 eggs	Manual cavatelli maker
	1 teaspoon kosher salt	

1. Spread the all-purpose flour and ¾ cup rice flour on a clean, dry work surface. Place the ricotta, eggs, salt, and pepper on top of the flour. Use your hands to gather the ingredients together and gently knead the dough into a 10 by 3-inch log. Let rest for 2 minutes.

2. Lightly dust a clean, dry work surface with rice flour. Cut the log into 4 equal pieces. Press each piece into an oval shape. Use a floured rolling pin to make uniformly shaped ¼-inch-thick ovals. Cut each oval into 1-inch-wide strips. Pile the strips one on top of the other with a sprinkling of rice flour between the layers.

3. Screw the cavatelli maker onto the edge of a cutting board or countertop. Feed the strips through the cavatelli maker. Store the cavatelli on a rice flour–covered baking sheet until ready for use.

STORAGE: *The cavatelli can be frozen for up to 2 weeks. To prepare them for the freezer, place them, dusted with rice flour, in a single layer on a baking sheet and freeze. Once frozen, place them one on top of the other in an airtight container. To thaw for cooking, place the cavatelli in a single layer on a baking sheet in the refrigerator for not more than 1 hour before cooking. Cook according to the recipe directions.*

ORECCHIETTE

ORECCHIETTE IS A TYPE OF PASTA FROM APULIA, AND ITS NAME IN ITALIAN SUGGESTS THAT IT RESEMBLES LITTLE EARS. ALTHOUGH THIS IS A FRESH DOUGH—AND ONE OF THE FEW THAT USES SEMOLINA FLOUR AND DOESN'T USE EGGS—IT IS SHAPED AND DRIED BEFORE COOKING. DRY ORECCHIETTE HOLDS SAUCES MORE SUCCESSFULLY THAN ORECCHIETTE COOKED WHEN STILL SOFT.

I DON'T USE VERY WET, SAUCY SAUCES WITH ORECCHIETTE—THEY TEND TO DROWN THE PASTA. I PREFER LIGHTER SAUCES: VEGETABLES THAT ARE SAUTÉED IN OLIVE OIL, OR RICOTTA CHEESE THAT'S TOSSED WITH THE ORECCHIETTE AND A STURDY VEGETABLE LIKE ASPARAGUS.

MAKES 2 POUNDS ORECCHIETTE | SERVES 4–6

2 cups all-purpose flour	1 cup water
2 cups semolina flour	Rice flour for dusting

1. Add the all-purpose flour, semolina flour, and water to the bowl of a food processor fitted with a metal blade. Pulse several times until the dough resembles large crumbs.

2. Turn out the dough onto a clean, dry, rice flour–dusted work surface. Gather the dough and knead it until it comes together and is smooth and elastic, about 5 minutes. Shape the dough into a 7 by 2-inch log.

3. Cut the log into 4 equal pieces. Lightly dust the work surface with rice flour. Roll each piece into a ¼-inch-diameter rope. While rolling, you may have to cut the rope into smaller sections as it gets longer. The dough should yield fourteen ½-inch ropes that are 9 to 12 inches long. Cut each rope into ¼-inch coins. Use a fingertip to make an indentation in the center of each coin. Let the orecchiette dry on a rice flour–covered baking sheet.

STORAGE: *The dough, tightly wrapped with plastic film, can be refrigerated for up to 2 days or frozen for up to 2 weeks. Defrost in the refrigerator. The dough will discolor slightly, but its flavor will not be affected. The dry orecchiette can be stored in an airtight container or plastic bag, not refrigerated (refrigeration will make them moist and gluey), for up to 2 days.*

CRESPELLE

CRESPELLE are thin Italian crepes or pancakes. They are used throughout Italy in many different dishes—some are savory, some are sweet.

At our Sfoglia restaurants, I use crespelle to make a rolled, stuffed pasta that I call manicotti. However, the word *manicotti* is not really used in Italy. Instead, the Italians call all pasta stuffed into a tubular shape *cannelloni* (see Filled Pasta, page 9). I also make folded, stuffed pasta called *fazzoletti*—handkerchiefs—with the crespelle. Sometimes, instead of using sheets of pasta for lasagne, I use crespelle.

Most of the recipes in this book that use crespelle call for sixteen crepes. This recipe makes approximately eighteen. The first two are generally considered the ones that season the pan.

MAKES SIXTEEN–EIGHTEEN 8-INCH CREPES

¼ pound (8 tablespoons) unsalted butter	3 eggs	1 teaspoon kosher salt
2 cups whole milk	1½ cups all-purpose flour	1 teaspoon sugar

1. Brown the butter in an 8-inch skillet over medium-high heat. Remove from the heat and reserve.

2. Whisk together the milk, eggs, all-purpose flour, salt, and sugar in a mixing bowl—there will be a few lumps. Quickly add the browned butter, whisking continuously. This should dissolve the lumps and create a smooth batter.

3. Place the butter-seasoned skillet over medium heat. Use a 2-ounce ladle or a ¼-cup measuring cup to add the batter to the center of the skillet. Tilt the pan from side to side to let the batter cover the bottom, not the sides, of the pan in a thin, even layer. Cook until the edges begin to brown, about 1 minute. Use a spatula to flip the crepe, then cook for 1 more minute. Pile the cooked crepes one on top of the other on a baking sheet or large platter until ready to use.

CUSCINETTI

THIS IS THE RECIPE THAT I'VE CHOSEN TO USE FOR SFOGLIA'S SIGNATURE RAVIOLI. IT IS INCLUDED HERE BECAUSE I ALWAYS MAKE *CUSCINETTI* THE SAME WAY—STUFFED WITH OUR OWN HOUSE-MADE GOAT'S MILK CHEESE AND COW'S MILK RICOTTA. THESE SIMPLE LITTLE PILLOWS ARE A PERFECT CONTRAST FOR MORE COMPLEX SAUCES. THERE ARE TWO RECIPES IN THIS BOOK THAT USE CUSCINETTI. IN ADDITION, THEY ARE WONDERFUL SAUCED WITH BROWN BUTTER AND SAGE, OR WITH THE SIMPLE TOMATO SAUCE SCIUÈ, SCIUÈ (PAGE 94).

MAKES 24–30 PIECES CUSCINETTI | SERVES 4–6

1 recipe Fresh Egg Pasta, cut for filled pasta (pages 2 and 9)

½ pound Goat's Milk Cheese (page 27)

½ pound whole milk ricotta

Rice flour for dusting

1. Fold together the goat's milk cheese and ricotta in a mixing bowl until combined.

2. Line up the pasta sheets, 2 at a time, on a clean, dry work surface. Starting 2 inches up from the bottom and ½ inch in from the sides of the sheets, place a rounded teaspoon of the cheese filling. Continue to place the filling every inch along the sheets. Use a pastry brush dipped in water to moisten the edges of the pasta sheets between the mounds of filling. Fold the pasta sheets over from the top to the bottom. Seal the cuscinetti by pressing down with your fingers, working from the filling out to the edges. Use a sharp knife or pastry wheel to cut down between the mounds of filling. Store the cuscinetti on a rice flour–covered baking sheet until ready to use.

STORAGE: *The cuscinetti can be kept frozen for up to 2 weeks. To prepare them for the freezer, place them, dusted with rice flour, in a single layer on a baking sheet and freeze. Once frozen, place them one on top of the other in an airtight container. There is no need to thaw before cooking. Cook according to the recipe directions.*

BRODO

M Y RECIPE FOR *BRODO*—WHICH IS A TWO-DAY PROJECT—IS SOMEWHERE BETWEEN A STOCK, WHICH IS COOKED WITH ROASTED BONES AND VEGETABLES FOR A LONG PERIOD OF TIME, AND A BROTH, WHICH IS COOKED WITH A WHOLE CHICKEN AND VEGETABLES FOR A SHORTER PERIOD OF TIME. I USE A WHOLE CHICKEN AND VEGETABLES AND COOK MY BRODO FOR THREE AND A HALF HOURS, THEREBY EXTRACTING ALL THE MARROW FROM THE CHICKEN BONES AND PRODUCING A RICH, GELATINOUS BROTH. THE BROTH CAN BE EATEN ON ITS OWN WITH TORTELLINI (PAGE 114) OR PASTA SCRAPS, OR USED AS AN INGREDIENT TO ADD FLAVOR AND DEPTH TO SAUCES AND SOUPS.

AFTER THIS BROTH HAS BEEN SIMMERING FOR ABOUT THIRTY MINUTES, YOU WILL NEED TO POUR OFF HALF OF THE LIQUID, INCLUDING THE IMPURITIES THAT HAVE FLOATED TO THE TOP, AND REPLACE IT WITH FRESH WATER. THE RESULT IS A CLEAR BROTH.

MAKES 2–2½ QUARTS BROTH

One whole 3-pound chicken

4 quarts water

2 unpeeled carrots, rinsed, cut into 1-inch pieces

2 ribs celery, rinsed, cut into 1-inch pieces

1 large onion, unpeeled, cut into 1-inch pieces

½ teaspoon freshly ground black pepper

2 teaspoons kosher salt

1. Place the chicken in a 5-quart stockpot. Cover with the water, bring to a boil, and cook for about 20 minutes. Lower the heat to medium and cook for 10 minutes more. Pour off half of the water. Add more water to come up to the level it was before. Turn up the heat to high. Add the carrots, celery, and onion, and bring to a boil. Lower the heat to medium high, which is a simmer, add the salt and pepper, and reduce until the liquid is at the top of the chicken, about 3½ hours. Let cool. Cover and refrigerate overnight.

2. The next day, remove the congealed fat that will have risen to the top of the broth. Bring the broth to room temperature. Strain into a large bowl. Place the chicken and vegetables into a colander and place over a large bowl so that they can release more liquid.

STORAGE: *The broth can be used immediately or frozen for up to 2 weeks in ½-pint, pint, or quart containers for future use.*

LIMONCELLO

THIS RECIPE COMES FROM AN UMBRIAN FRIEND OF OURS WHOSE MOTHER IS FROM NAPLES. NAPLES IS GENERALLY RECOGNIZED AS THE HOME OF A LIQUEUR CALLED LIMONCELLO, ALTHOUGH IT'S MADE IN ALMOST ALL THE SEASIDE TOWNS OF ITALY WHERE LEMONS GROW IN PROFUSION.

OUR FRIEND MARIDA INSISTS THAT THE LEMONS THAT ARE USED FOR HER RECIPE BE PLUMP AND ORGANIC. SHE CLAIMS THAT PLUMP LEMONS SIGNAL THAT THE SKIN IS OILY AND, THEREFORE, MORE FLAVORFUL. SHE SPECIFIES ORGANIC BECAUSE THE OUTSIDE ZEST IS WHAT IS USED, AND IT SHOULD BE AS FREE OF ADDED CHEMICALS AS POSSIBLE. MARIDA ALSO RECOMMENDS THAT AT LEAST ONE OF THE FIVE LEMONS CALLED FOR IN THIS RECIPE BE GREENER, OR LESS RIPE, THAN THE OTHERS BECAUSE THERE'S EVEN MORE FLAVOR IN THEM.

I LIKE TO USE A SPLASH OF THIS LIQUEUR TO ENHANCE SAUCES THAT INCLUDE LEMON AS ONE OF THEIR INGREDIENTS, LIKE THE FETTUCCINE, LEMON CREAM, TOASTED ALMONDS (PAGE 34); LINGUINE, MONKFISH POLPETTE, TOMATO, PARSLEY (PAGE 70); LEMON RICOTTA GNOCCHI, NANTUCKET BAY SCALLOPS, RAISINS, SLICED PROSCIUTTO (PAGE 159); AND LEMON RISOTTO, ROASTED BONE MARROW, LIMONCELLO (PAGE 176).

MAKES 1½ PINTS

5 plump organic lemons	2 cups grain alcohol or 100 proof vodka	1 cup water
		2 cups sugar

1. Carefully grate the zest, the yellow part of the lemon peel, avoiding the white pith. Add the zest and alcohol to a glass quart jar or bottle and close tightly. Store in a cool, dry place for 6 to 10 days.

2. After 6 to 10 days, make a simple syrup. Add the water and sugar to a saucepan over medium-high heat. After the sugar has completely dissolved, cook for approximately 3 more minutes. Let cool.

3. Strain the syrup into the jar that holds the lemon mixture. Stir to combine. Close the lid tightly. Store in a dark, cool, dry place for 30 days.

4. After 30 days, pour the liquid through a fine-mesh strainer into a bowl. Add the limoncello back into the jar or a decorative bottle. Store in the refrigerator or freezer for future use.

preserved LEMONS

At our Sfoglia restaurants, we use chopped preserved lemons as a garnish for finished pasta, fish, and side dishes. We also use them in pasta fillings and sauces, and for the Linguine, Monkfish Polpette, Tomato, Parsley (page 70).

There are many different ways to make preserved lemons. This one is a two-step process that I adapted from my former New York Sfoglia chef de cuisine, Molly Smith, who brought the recipe with her when she came to work with us.

I suggest that you double or triple this recipe and keep a jar handy in your pantry.

MAKES 6 WHOLE PRESERVED LEMONS

6 lemons	3 quarts water	2 cups sugar
8 cups kosher salt	20 sprigs fresh thyme	

1. Make 4 equally spaced vertical cuts to the flesh on each lemon. Bury the lemons in the salt in a large glass or plastic container with a tight-fitting lid. Store in a cool, dry place for 10 days.

2. Pull the lemons out of the salt. Add the water, thyme, sugar, and 2 cups of the lemon salt to a 5-quart stockpot. Bring the mixture to a boil. Add the lemons and bring the brine back to a boil. Turn off the heat. Let cool.

3. Place the lemons in an airtight container. Cover with the brine (you may not need to use all of it) and refrigerate for 2 weeks before using.

STORAGE: *The lemons can be refrigerated in an airtight container for up to 6 months.*

goat's milk CHEESE

HEN WE OPENED OUR SFOGLIA RESTAURANT ON NANTUCKET, COLLEEN IMMEDIATELY BEGAN TO LOOK FOR A SOURCE FOR FRESH MILK TO MAKE HER GELATO. WE HAD ALREADY ESTABLISHED A RELATIONSHIP WITH RAY OWEN, A LOCAL FARMER FROM WHOM WE GOT CHICKEN EGGS. BECAUSE RAY HAD BEEN A DAIRY FARMER ON THE MAINLAND BEFORE HE MOVED TO THE ISLAND, COLLEEN ASKED HIM IF HE KNEW ANYONE IN MASSACHUSETTS WHO COULD SUPPLY FRESH MILK. HIS ANSWER TO THAT QUESTION CAME WHEN HE WALKED INTO OUR KITCHEN ONE DAY WITH THE NEWS THAT HIS SONS, WHO HAD TAKEN OVER HIS MAINLAND FARM, HAD SENT HIM A FEMALE GOAT AND HE WANTED TO BREED IT. HE WONDERED IF WE'D BE INTERESTED IN FRESH GOAT'S MILK. COLLEEN DECIDED TO ADAPT HER GELATO RECIPE FOR IT. PLEASED WITH THE RESULTS, SHE BEGAN TO EXPERIMENT WITH MAKING CHEESE. THIS, TOO, WAS A SUCCESS. TO MEET OUR DEMAND FOR MORE MILK, RAY KEPT BREEDING GOATS.

ONCE WE HAD THIS INFALLIBLE RECIPE FOR GOAT'S MILK CHEESE, WE REALIZED THAT THE CHEESE, WITH ITS DISTINCT TANGY FLAVOR AND CREAMY TEXTURE, COULD BE ADDED TO OUR RAVIOLI AND LASAGNE FILLINGS AND TO CHEESE AND VEGETABLE TERRINES, AND USED AS A GARNISH ON EVERYTHING FROM PASTAS TO ANTIPASTI TO SIDE DISHES. IF YOU DON'T HAVE THE TIME THAT'S REQUIRED TO MAKE THIS RECIPE, SUBSTITUTE WITH A STORE-BOUGHT, SOFT GOAT'S MILK CHEESE.

MAKES ABOUT 2 POUNDS CHEESE

1 gallon fresh goat's milk	$\frac{1}{16}$ teaspoon liquid mesophilic DVI (see Resources, page 194)	Cheesecloth
$\frac{1}{4}$ teaspoon powdered mesophilic DVI (see Resources, page 194)		

1. Heat the goat's milk in a large nonreactive saucepan over medium heat until the temperature reaches exactly 75°F on an instant-read thermometer. Remove from the heat.

2. Add the powdered and liquid mesophilic DVI to a small bowl. Add 2 tablespoons of the warm goat's milk to the bowl and thoroughly combine. Add the mixture to the rest of the milk in the saucepan. Let sit, covered and undisturbed, overnight.

3. Cut the set-up cheese into quarters. Completely cover a colander with a double layer of cheesecloth. Place the colander over a large bowl. Carefully pour the cheese quarters through the colander. Let sit until all the whey, or liquid, has been strained (see Note). Place the cheese in an airtight container.

STORAGE: *The cheese can be stored in the refrigerator for up to 2 weeks and in the freezer for up to 1 month.*

NOTE: *If the whey that you've collected is very cloudy, then you might try to make ricotta (see Variation). If not, discard.*

VARIATION:

1. To make ricotta, heat the whey in a large nonreactive saucepan over medium heat until the temperature reaches 180°F on an instant-read thermometer—almost at a boil. Remove from the heat and leave at room temperature for 12 to 18 hours. The whey should separate into curds.

2. Line a colander with a double layer of cheesecloth. Place the colander over a large bowl. Carefully pour the ricotta through the colander. Let sit until all the liquid has been strained. Place the ricotta in an airtight container.

STORAGE: *The ricotta can be stored in the refrigerator for up to 2 weeks and in the freezer for up to 1 month.*

PASTA WATER

YOU HAVE TO HAVE A POT OF BOILING WATER BEFORE YOU CAN EVEN THINK ABOUT COOKING PASTA.

5 quarts water	2 tablespoons kosher salt	2 pounds fresh or 1 pound dry pasta from your selected recipe

Seasoning the water with salt is an important part of my "making pasta" philosophy. I believe that each component of a dish that's cooked separately needs to be seasoned separately. When the pasta begins to cook in salted water and releases its starch, it produces yet another ingredient, pasta water. There are many recipes in this book where I ask for the addition of this starchy water to the sauce. Adding it ensures a good marriage between the pasta and the sauce. When cooked pasta is added to the sauce, it will absorb the extra pasta water, *NOT* the sauce. The sauce will then coat the pasta.

(Note: I think that it's important to use a wire-mesh skimmer or tongs to remove pasta from the pot. When wet pasta is added directly into the sauce, both components join to become the one dish.)

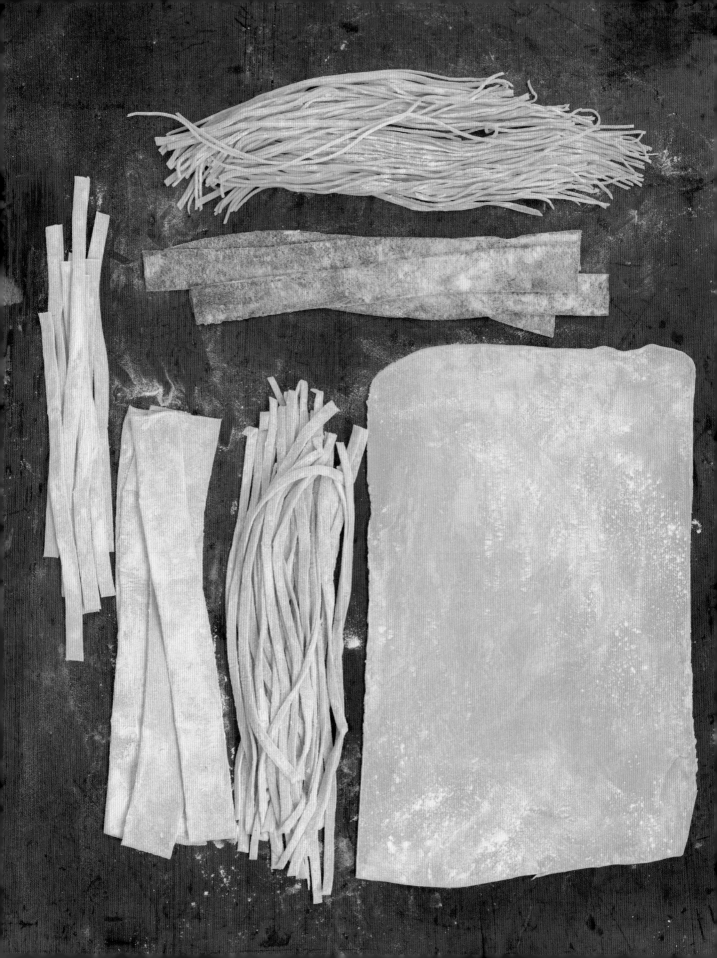

fresh PASTA

I think of fresh pasta as something special, but something not just for special occasions. Although you may be intimidated by the thought of making it, niente paura, *Have no fear. With my method—which uses a food processor to make the dough and an electric pasta maker to roll out the* sfoglia *(the uncut sheet of pasta)—you'll always be able to treat yourself to exceptional meals. The results of your efforts will give you strong yet tender pasta capable of being tossed with even the most complex sauces.*

PAPPARDELLE alla bolognese

At my second full-fledged chef's position at the Galleria Italiana in Boston, the owners were two women from Abruzzi. While I was familiar with the classic version of *ragù alla Bolognese*—chopped beef, carrots, celery, onions, and tomatoes—I noticed that Rita and Marisa added chicken livers to their version. When I started making my own Bolognese sauce, I used a combination of veal, pork, and lamb instead of the beef for an even more complex flavor. I kept Rita and Marisa's chicken livers and added some sweet Italian sausage because my grandmother used it in her Sunday Ragù (page 62) to deepen and enrich the sauce's flavor.

MAKES 2 QUARTS SAUCE | ENOUGH FOR 2 BATCHES SERVING 4–6

DAY ONE: FOR THE BOLOGNESE SAUCE

2 tablespoons grape seed oil

2 cloves garlic, thinly sliced

½ pound chicken livers, pureed in a food processor until smooth

1 pound sweet Italian sausages, casings removed

1 sprig fresh rosemary

1 pound ground pork

1 pound ground lamb

1 pound ground veal

½ cup full-bodied red wine

One 1-pound 12-ounce can peeled whole San Marzano tomatoes

3 cups water swirled in the tomato can

DAY TWO: FOR 4 TO 6 SERVINGS

1 recipe Fresh Egg Pasta, cut for pappardelle (pages 2 and 8)

4 cups Bolognese sauce (above; see storage)

1 cup heavy cream

1 teaspoon kosher salt

¼ teaspoon freshly ground black pepper

½ cup Pasta Water (page 29)

Grated Parmesan cheese, optional garnish

1. **FOR THE BOLOGNESE SAUCE:** Preheat the oven to 400°F. Heat the grape seed oil in a large heavy-bottomed, ovenproof casserole over medium-high heat for 1 minute. Add the garlic and chicken livers and cook, stirring occasionally, until the pink disappears from the livers. Add the sausages and break them up with a wooden spoon. Cook until the pink disappears from the sausage. Add the rosemary, pork, lamb, and veal and stir continuously to combine. Cook until the pink completely disappears from all the meats, about 10 to 12 minutes. Add the red wine and reduce for 5 minutes. Add the tomatoes and water. Bring to a boil.

2. Place the casserole in the oven and cook, uncovered, for 3 hours. Stir from time to time. It's important to fold the top of the mixture into the bottom to ensure the marriage of flavors. Let cool. Refrigerate, covered, overnight.

3. **FOR SERVING:** Remove the Bolognese sauce from the refrigerator.

4. Bring a large pot of salted water (see page 29) to a boil. Remove the rosemary from the Bolognese sauce. Add the 4 cups sauce to a 10-inch skillet over medium heat. Add the cream, salt, and pepper and bring to a simmer.

5. Add the pappardelle to the boiling water and cook until they float to the top. Cook for 2 more minutes. Add the ½ cup pasta water to the sauce. Use a wire-mesh skimmer or tongs to remove the pasta from the pot and place it directly into the skillet with the sauce. Stir to evenly coat the pappardelle with the sauce.

6. Serve immediately with a garnish of Parmesan cheese, if desired.

STORAGE: *The remaining quart of sauce can be stored in the refrigerator for up to 5 days or frozen for up to 2 months. To freeze in smaller portions, place the sauce in ½-pint or pint containers. To serve, adjust the cream and other seasonings accordingly.*

FETTUCCINE, lemon cream, toasted almonds

HEN I BEGIN TO THINK ABOUT HOW TO PUT INGREDIENTS TOGETHER FOR A DISH, ONE OF THE THINGS THAT I LIKE TO CONSIDER IS INGREDIENTS THAT GROW TOGETHER. IT SEEMS TO ME THAT THE SAME ATTRACTION THAT THEY HAVE FOR ONE ANOTHER IN THE EARTH SHOULD TRANSLATE TO THE PLATE. WHILE LEMONS AND ALMONDS ARE NOT HARVESTED AT THE SAME TIME OF THE YEAR, THEY DO GROW IN THE SAME ORCHARDS.

THIS IS MY WINTERTIME VERSION OF SPAGHETTI AL LIMONE, ALMOND PESTO, GRATED RICOTTA SALATA (PAGE 77). BY MAKING A LEMON CREAM AND SERVING IT WITH FRESH PASTA AND CHOPPED ROASTED ALMONDS, YOU END UP WITH A SUBSTANTIAL DISH, PERFECT FOR THE COLD WEATHER.

HERE'S AN EXAMPLE OF A RECIPE THAT COULD BE ENHANCED BY A SPLASH OF LIMONCELLO (PAGE 23).

SERVES 4–6

1 recipe Fresh Egg Pasta, cut for fettuccine (pages 2 and 8)

2 whole lemons, cut in half

¼ cup grape seed oil

4 sprigs fresh thyme

1½ cups whole almonds

2 cups heavy cream

½ teaspoon kosher salt

¼ teaspoon freshly ground black pepper

½ cup Pasta Water (page 29)

Splash of Limoncello (page 23), optional

1. Preheat the oven to 350°F. Place the lemons flesh side down in a glass or ceramic baking dish. Cover with the grape seed oil and thyme. Bake until the lemons are tender and beginning to brown and the oil is bubbling, about 1 hour.

2. Place the almonds evenly on a baking sheet with sides. Place in the oven with the lemons until you begin to smell them and they are browned, about 16 to 18 minutes.

3. Place the cooked lemons, their juices, and the cream in a nonreactive saucepan over high heat. Bring to a boil. Immediately reduce the heat to a simmer and cook until the cream coats the back of a spoon, about 10 to 12 minutes.

4. Bring a large pot of salted water (see page 29) to a boil. Strain the cream sauce into a 10-inch skillet.

5. Add the almonds to the bowl of a food processor fitted with a metal blade and coarsely chop. Add the chopped almonds, salt, and pepper to the skillet. Add the fettuccine to the boiling water and cook until they float to the top. Cook for 2 more minutes. Add the ½ cup pasta water to the cream sauce and turn up the heat to medium.

6. Use a wire-mesh skimmer or tongs to remove the pasta from the pot and place it directly into the skillet with the sauce. Add a splash of Limoncello, if desired. Stir to thoroughly coat the fettuccine with the sauce.

7. Serve immediately.

DUCK EGG FETTUCCINE, braised duck, wild mushrooms, currants

I LIKE THE HARMONY THAT'S CREATED BY PAIRING DUCK EGG PASTA WITH A BRAISED DUCK SAUCE. IT KEEPS EVERYTHING IN THE FAMILY. I PREFER MOULARD DUCK, A HYBRID OF THE WIDELY USED PEKINS, OR LONG ISLAND DUCKS, AND THE MUSCOVY. THE FLESH IS VERY TENDER. THE COOKING TIME OF THE BREASTS WILL DEPEND ON THEIR SIZE.

WITH THE GAMY FLAVOR OF THE DUCK, I KNEW THAT I HAD TO ADD SOMETHING SWEET AND FRUITY TO PROVIDE CONTRAST. THE CURRANTS TURNED OUT TO BE JUST THE RIGHT THING.

SERVES 4–6

1 recipe Duck Egg Pasta, cut for fettuccine (pages 4 and 8)

3 pounds duck breasts

½ pound assorted wild mushrooms, such as oyster, trumpet, and mitaki, cleaned and trimmed

½ cup dried currants

1 cup dry white wine

4 cups water

½ cup Pasta Water (page 29)

Grated pecorino Romano, optional garnish

1. Place a heavy-bottomed casserole over high heat. When the pot is smoking hot, add the duck breasts fat side down. Turn the heat to medium. Slowly, taking care not to brown too quickly, render the fat by more than half, 10 to 40 minutes, depending on the size of the breasts. Remove the breasts from the casserole and pour off almost all the fat, leaving just enough to coat the bottom of the pot. Turn the heat back to high, add the mushrooms, and sauté for 2 minutes. Add the currants and stir to combine. Return the duck breasts flesh side down to the pot (make sure you scrape in the juices that may have been released from the breasts while they were resting). Add the white wine and reduce by half, about 12 to 15 minutes. Add the water and bring to a boil. Lower the heat to a simmer and cook until the duck is fork-tender, 45 minutes to 1½ hours, depending on the size of the breasts.

2. Remove the breasts from the sauce and let cool. When cool enough to touch, remove the skin. Thinly slice the duck into pieces no larger than 2-inch squares. Return to the casserole and stir to combine.

3. Bring a large pot of salted water (see page 29) to a boil. Add the fettuccine to the boiling water and cook until they float to the top. Cook for 2 more minutes. Add the ½ cup pasta water to the sauce.

4. Use a wire-mesh skimmer or tongs to remove the pasta from the pot and place it directly into the sauce. Stir together to combine.

5. Serve immediately with grated pecorino Romano, if desired.

DUCK EGG TAJARIN, salsa di tartufo nero, pecorino romano

URING OUR STAY NEAR THE PIEDMONTESE TOWN OF ALBA, I LEARNED HOW TO MAKE *TAJARIN*, THE LOCAL DIALECT FOR TAGLIATELLE. IN ALBA, TAJARIN ARE CLASSICALLY DRESSED WITH BUTTER AND TOPPED WITH A MOUNTAIN OF FINELY SHAVED LOCAL WHITE TRUFFLES. SOME TIME LATER, WHEN COLLEEN AND I WENT TO WORK AT IL POGGIO DEI PETTI ROSSI IN THE LITTLE TOWN OF BEVAGNA, I LEARNED ABOUT THE *TARTUFO NERO*, BLACK TRUFFLES, INDIGENOUS TO UMBRIA. I'VE CHOSEN BLACK TRUFFLES FOR THIS SAUCE BECAUSE THEY ARE STURDIER THAN THE VERY DELICATE WHITE ONES AND ARE ALWAYS COOKED FOR CONSUMPTION. I THINK THAT THE PRESERVED TRUFFLES TASTE A LITTLE BIT MORE LIKE MUSHROOMS THAN FRESH TRUFFLES. HOWEVER, IF YOU CAN'T GET FRESH BLACK TRUFFLES, THE JARRED ONES, WITH THEIR FLAVOR HIGH-LIGHTED BY THE ADDITION OF ANCHOVIES, GARLIC, AND RED PEPPER FLAKES, MAKE A FINE SAUCE.

SERVES 4–6

1 recipe Duck Egg Pasta, cut for tagliatelle (pages 4 and 8)

½ cup grape seed oil

2 ounces fresh or jarred black truffles, coarsely chopped

1 clove garlic, cut in half

2 small anchovy fillets, rinsed

¼ teaspoon red pepper flakes

¼ teaspoon freshly ground black pepper

1 cup grated pecorino Romano, plus more for serving

¼ cup Pasta Water (page 29)

1. Add the grape seed oil, truffles, garlic, anchovies, and red pepper flakes to a small saucepan over high heat and bring to a boil. Turn off the heat. Let cool.

2. Puree the truffle mixture in the jar of a blender. Add the pureed mixture to a 10-inch skillet.

3. Bring a large pot of salted water (see page 29) to a boil. Add the tagliatelle to the boiling water and cook until they float to the top. Cook for 2 more minutes. Add the black pepper and 1 cup grated pecorino Romano to the truffle sauce.

4. Use a wire-mesh skimmer or tongs to remove the pasta from the pot and place it directly into the skillet. Add the ¼ cup pasta water. Stir to thoroughly combine the tagliatelle with the sauce. Cook for 1 more minute.

5. Serve immediately with a garnish of grated pecorino Romano.

TAGLIATELLE, sea urchins, sweet 100 cherry tomatoes, parsley

OU'LL FIND THAT THIS DISH IS SIMILAR IN STYLE TO THE TAGLIATELLE, BOTTARGA, ROASTED CHERRY TOMATOES, PARSLEY (PAGE 40), BUT THE ADDITION OF SEA URCHINS LENDS A MUCH DIFFERENT FLAVOR. IN THE STATES, SEA URCHINS ARE HARVESTED ON BOTH THE EAST AND WEST COASTS. EAST COAST SEA URCHINS TEND TO BE SALTIER THAN THE SWEETER WEST COAST ONES, WHICH I PREFER WITH THIS RECIPE BECAUSE THEY COMPLEMENT THE SWEET 100 TOMATOES SO WELL.

SERVES 4–6

1 recipe Fresh Egg Pasta, cut for tagliatelle (pages 2 and 8)

½ cup olive oil

2¼ cups Sweet 100 cherry tomatoes, cut in half

1 clove garlic, thinly sliced

½ pound fresh sea urchins

½ cup coarsely chopped flat-leaf parsley

2 tablespoons fresh lemon juice

1. Heat the olive oil in a 10-inch skillet over medium-low heat. When the oil is warm, add the tomatoes and garlic and raise the heat to medium. Agitate the pan from time to time so that the tomatoes won't stick to the bottom of the pan.

2. Bring a large pot of salted water (see page 29) to a boil.

3. When the tomatoes have blistered, add the sea urchins and parsley. Turn off the heat. Add the lemon juice.

4. Add the tagliatelle to the boiling water and cook until they float to the top. Cook for 2 minutes. Use a wire-mesh skimmer or tongs to remove the pasta from the pot and place it directly into the sauce. Stir to combine.

5. Serve immediately.

TAGLIATELLE, bottarga, roasted cherry tomatoes, parsley

BOTTARGA, EITHER *BOTTARGA DI MUGGINE*——THE CURED EGGS OF MULLET——OR *BOTTARGA DI TONNO*——THE CURED EGGS OF TUNA——GIVES THIS SIMPLE DISH ITS DISTINCTIVE FLAVOR. IT IS SOLD IN TWO DIFFERENT FORMS: THE WHOLE EGG SAC, WHICH CAN BE SHAVED, OR GROUND, CALLED *MACINATO*.

I LOVE BOTTARGA'S NUTTY FLAVOR AND GRAINY TEXTURE. I THINK THAT IT WORKS BEST IN COMBINATION WITH OTHER INGREDIENTS THAT HAVE THEIR OWN PARTICULAR FLAVORS, LIKE TOMATOES AND PARSLEY——INGREDIENTS THAT ARE OFTEN USED WITH FISH IN THE ITALIAN KITCHEN.

SERVES 4–6

1 recipe Fresh Egg Pasta, cut for tagliatelle (pages 2 and 8)

1½ pounds large cherry tomatoes, cut in half

¼ cup olive oil

½ teaspoon kosher salt

⅛ teaspoon freshly ground black pepper

½ cup extra virgin olive oil

1 clove garlic, thinly sliced

¾ cup coarsely chopped flat-leaf parsley

½ cup ground bottarga

¼ cup fresh lemon juice

1. Preheat the oven to 350°F. Combine the tomatoes, olive oil, salt, and pepper in a large mixing bowl. Toss to thoroughly coat the tomatoes. Place flesh side up on a baking sheet with sides. Cook in the oven until the tomatoes are shriveled and slightly browned, about 1 hour.

2. Bring a large pot of salted water (see page 29) to a boil.

3. Add the cooked tomatoes, extra virgin olive oil, garlic, and parsley to a 10-inch skillet. Turn on the heat to medium. Agitate the pan from time to time to keep the tomatoes from sticking to the bottom of the pan. Add the bottarga and toast for about 4 to 5 minutes. Turn off the heat. Stir in the lemon juice. Remove the pan to a cool burner.

4. Add the tagliatelle to the boiling water and cook until they float to the top. Cook for 2 more minutes. Use a wire-mesh skimmer or tongs to remove the pasta from the pot and place it directly into the skillet with the sauce. Stir to combine the pasta and sauce.

5. Serve immediately.

SPAGHETTI, winter seafood, saffron, parsley

ONE SUMMER, MY BOSSES RITA AND MARISA AT THE GALLERIA ITALIANA IN BOSTON TOOK ME ON AN INSPIRATIONAL VISIT TO THEIR HOME REGION OF ABRUZZI ON ITALY'S ADRIATIC COAST. THERE, IN THE SEASIDE TOWN OF PESCARA, WE ATE AT ONE OF THEIR FAVORITE RESTAURANTS. WE DIDN'T HAVE TO *ORDER* FOOD; WE WERE SERVED THE DISHES CHOSEN BY THE RESTAURANT'S OWNER. ONE DISH WAS AN ABRUZZESE VERSION OF *BRODETTO*—THE ITALIAN BOUILLABAISSE—WHICH WAS ACCOMPANIED BY SAFFRON MAYONNAISE INSTEAD OF THE CLASSIC AIOLI. SAFFRON GROWS IN ABRUZZI, MAKING IT A FREQUENTLY USED INGREDIENT THROUGHOUT THE REGION.

THIS PASTA, WITH FRESH SEAFOOD AND SAFFRON, IS A DIRECT DESCENDANT OF THE BRODETTO THAT WE HAD IN PESCARA YEARS AGO. I'VE ADDED THE AVAILABLE-ONLY-IN-THE-WINTERTIME NANTUCKET BAY SCALLOPS IN HONOR OF OUR ISLAND RESTAURANT.

BECAUSE THE SEAFOOD IS COOKED AND SERVED WITH ITS SHELLS INTACT, YOU'LL FIND IT EASIER, AND MORE ENJOYABLE, TO EAT IT WITH YOUR HANDS.

SERVES 4–6

1 recipe Fresh Egg Pasta, cut for spaghetti (pages 2 and 8)

2 tablespoons grape seed oil

1 clove garlic, thinly sliced

1 teaspoon saffron threads

18 Manila clams

12 mussels

12 shrimps, heads on

1 cup dry white wine

1 cup Pasta Water (page 29)

1 pound Nantucket bay scallops

1 cup loosely packed flat-leaf parsley

1. Add the grape seed oil, garlic, and saffron to a 10-inch skillet. Turn on the heat to high. Immediately add the clams and mussels. Agitate the pan from time to time. When the edges of the garlic turn golden, about 1 minute, add the shrimps. When the shrimps start to turn pink, add the white wine. Stir to combine. Lower the heat to medium.

2. Bring a large pot of salted water (see page 29) to a boil. Add the spaghetti to the boiling water. Add the 1 cup pasta water and the scallops to the skillet and cover. After the spaghetti float to the top, cook for 2 more minutes.

3. Use a wire-mesh skimmer or tongs to remove the spaghetti from the pot and place them in a warm shallow serving dish. Toss with the seafood sauce and parsley. Alternatively, serve individual plates.

4. Serve immediately.

SPAGHETTI, tomato, cloves, thyme

HEN THE KITCHEN FILLS WITH THE SPICY AROMA OF CLOVES COOKING IN THIS
SAUCE, I'M ALWAYS REMINDED OF THE HOLIDAYS. THE VERY-EASY-TO-MAKE FRESH
SPAGHETTI AND SIMPLE TOMATO SAUCE ARE JUST THE RIGHT THING FOR A SPECIAL
MEAL WHEN YOU'RE BUSY DOING OTHER THINGS AT THAT TIME OF THE YEAR.

SERVES 4–6

1 recipe Fresh Egg Pasta, cut for
spaghetti (pages 2 and 8)

2 tablespoons grape seed oil

2 tablespoons fresh thyme leaves

1 clove garlic, thinly sliced

1 teaspoon ground cloves

4 cups peeled whole San Marzano
tomatoes, (see Pantry, page xvii),
passed through a food mill

1 cup water

1 teaspoon kosher salt

¼ teaspoon freshly ground black
pepper

1. Add the grape seed oil, thyme, garlic, and cloves to a 10-inch skillet. Turn on
the heat to high. When the edges of the garlic turn golden, about 1 minute, add the
tomato puree and water. Cook, stirring occasionally, for 5 minutes. Lower the heat
to medium and add the salt and pepper.

2. Bring a large pot of salted water (see page 29) to a boil. Add the spaghetti to the
boiling water and cook until they float to the top. Cook for 2 more minutes. Use a
wire-mesh skimmer or tongs to remove the pasta from the pot and place it directly
into the skillet with the sauce. Stir to combine. Cook for 1 more minute.

3. Serve immediately.

44 PASTA SFOGLIA

ORECCHIETTE, spicy tomato, peas, 2-minute calamari

ONE OF OUR REGULAR SFOGLIA NANTUCKET CUSTOMERS, DAVID GOODMAN, IS NOT ONLY A DEDICATED FISHERMAN, BUT A COLUMNIST WHO WRITES ABOUT HIS FAVORITE ACTIVITY IN HIS "FISH FINDERS" COLUMN FOR THE LOCAL NEWSPAPER. I CREATED THIS DISH AFTER HE BROUGHT ME HIS CALAMARI—SQUID—CATCH LATE ONE SPRINGTIME EVENING. IT'S A GIVEN THAT SPICES AND CALAMARI GO TOGETHER. THE FRESH, SWEET SPRINGTIME PEAS SEEMED TO BE THE NATURAL NEXT INGREDIENT. ORECCHIETTE WERE THE RIGHT CHOICE TO COMPLEMENT THE CALAMARI RINGS AND THE PEAS.

SERVES 4–6

1 recipe Orecchiette (page 18)

2 tablespoons grape seed oil

1 clove garlic, thinly sliced

½ teaspoon red pepper flakes

2 cups shelled fresh or frozen peas

4 cups peeled whole San Marzano tomatoes, passed through a food mill

1 cup water

2 teaspoons kosher salt

1 pound calamari, cut into ¼-inch rings, tentacles included

1. Add the grape seed oil and garlic to a 10-inch skillet. Turn on the heat to high. When the edges of the garlic turn golden, about 1 minute, add the red pepper flakes and peas. Cook for 2 minutes. Add the tomato puree, water, and salt and cook until reduced by half, about 15 to 20 minutes. Lower the heat to medium.

2. Bring a large pot of salted water (see page 29) to a boil. Add the orecchiette to the boiling water. When the pasta has cooked for 8 minutes and it has 2 minutes left to cook, add the calamari to the sauce. After *exactly* 2 minutes, use a wire-mesh skimmer to remove the orecchiette from the pot and place them directly into the sauce. Stir with the heat still on to thoroughly coat the orecchiette with the sauce.

3. Serve immediately.

ORECCHIETTE, asparagus, fresh lemon ricotta

THIS DISH IS PERFECT FOR LATE SPRINGTIME, WHEN ASPARAGUS ARE AT THE HEIGHT OF THEIR SEASON. BECAUSE OF THE WAY THE SAUCE IS MADE, THEN COMBINED WITH THE PASTA, IT'S ALWAYS SERVED WARM OR AT ROOM TEMPERATURE.

IN THE SUMMERTIME, WHEN TENDER ZUCCHINI FIRST APPEAR AT THE LOCAL FARM STANDS ON NANTUCKET AND AT THE NEW YORK CITY GREENMARKETS, I SUBSTITUTE ZUCCHINI FOR THE ASPARAGUS TO MAKE AN EQUALLY APPEALING DISH.

SERVES 4–6

1 recipe Orecchiette (page 18)	1½ pounds whole milk ricotta	¼ teaspoon freshly ground black pepper; plus more for serving, optional
1 pound medium asparagus, woody ends removed, peeled to the bud ends, and cut into 1-inch pieces	2 lemons, zest from 1, juice from both	
	2 teaspoons kosher salt	

1. Bring a large pot of salted water (see page 29) to a boil. Add the orecchiette to the boiling water. Cook for 5 minutes. Add the asparagus and cook for 5 more minutes.

2. Add the ricotta, lemon zest, lemon juice, salt, and pepper to a large mixing bowl. Stir to combine.

3. Use a wire-mesh skimmer to remove the orecchiette and asparagus from the pot and place them directly into the bowl containing the sauce. Carefully fold together.

4. Serve immediately with freshly ground black pepper, if desired.

WHOLE WHEAT SPAGHETTI, artichokes, bottarga di muggine, pine nuts

E ATE LOTS OF ARTICHOKES WHEN WE WERE VISITING COLLEEN'S DISTANT RELATIVES IN SICILY IN THE COASTAL TOWN OF TERMINI IMERESE, ABOUT AN HOUR EAST OF PALERMO. MANY TIMES THE ARTICHOKES WERE INCLUDED IN SEAFOOD PREPARATIONS.

BECAUSE BOTTARGA AND WHOLE WHEAT PASTA ARE BOTH NUTTY AND GRITTY, I LIKED THE IDEA OF PAIRING THE TWO. THE ADDITION OF ARTICHOKES AND PINE NUTS BRINGS BACK GOOD MEMORIES OF OUR DAYS ON THE SICILIAN COAST.

SERVES 4–6

1 recipe Whole Wheat Pasta, cut for spaghetti (pages 5 and 8)	5 whole artichokes	2 tablespoons ground bottarga di muggine
Juice of 2 lemons	1 cup pine nuts	
	¼ cup extra virgin olive oil	

1. **PREP THE ARTICHOKES:** Add the juice of 1 lemon to a large bowl of cool water. Working with one artichoke at a time, cut the stem away from the base. Remove the outside leaves by bending them backward and pulling down; they'll snap at the "meaty" point of the leaf. Pull away the leaves until you see only pale green ones. Use a very sharp knife to cut away the remaining leaf tops. Quarter the artichoke and cut out the fuzzy choke. Use the same sharp knife to cut each quarter into thin slices. Immediately add the artichoke slices to the lemon water in order to prevent them from turning brown.

2. Preheat the oven to 350°F.

3. Place the pine nuts on a baking sheet with sides. Toast until golden, about 5 to 7 minutes.

4. Cook the artichokes slices in boiling water until tender, about 5 to 7 minutes. Drain. Add the extra virgin olive oil and bottarga to a 10-inch skillet over medium-high heat. Toast the bottarga for 1 minute. Add the artichokes and cook for 1 minute. Add the toasted pine nuts and the juice of the remaining lemon. Turn off the heat.

5. Bring a large pot of salted water (see page 29) to a boil. Add the spaghetti and cook until they float to the top. Cook for 2 more minutes. Use a wire-mesh skimmer or tongs to remove the spaghetti from the pot and place them directly into the skillet with the sauce. Stir together to combine.

6. Serve immediately.

WHOLE WHEAT SPAGHETTI, cabbage, wild mushrooms, guanciale, caraway

DURING MY CHILDHOOD, JUST AS SUNDAY MEALS WERE EATEN AT BIG NONNA'S, MY GREAT-GRANDMOTHER'S HOME, SATURDAY MEALS, ESPECIALLY IN THE SUMMERTIME, WERE HELD AT MY HUNGARIAN GRANDMOTHER'S HOME. THE WARM-WEATHER MEAL USUALLY CENTERED AROUND MEAT ROASTED OVER AN OUTDOOR GRILL. I REMEMBER THAT THERE WAS ALWAYS A BIG HUNK OF SKEWERED SMOKED PORK FAT SET OVER THE GRILL. WE'D CUP A PIECE OF RYE BREAD IN OUR HANDS AND HOLD IT UNDER THE DRIPPING FAT. THEN WE'D LOAD THE BREAD WITH ONIONS AND PEPPERS FOR THE BEST SANDWICH IMAGINABLE.

BECAUSE I LIKE TO TURN EVERY FOOD COMBINATION I ENCOUNTER INTO A PASTA DISH, IT WASN'T TOO DIFFICULT FOR ME TO START WITH WHOLE WHEAT SPAGHETTI AND ADD CARAWAY SEEDS, THEN SMOKY, SALTY *GUANCIALE*—CURED PORK JOWL—TO QUICKLY RE-CREATE ANOTHER FOOD MEMORY.

SERVES 4–6

1 recipe Whole Wheat Pasta, cut for spaghetti (pages 5 and 8)

1 tablespoon grape seed oil

½ pound guanciale, cut into ¼-inch dice (see Resources, page 194)

1 pound assorted mushrooms, such as hedgehogs, shiitakes, and oysters, cleaned, trimmed, and broken into pieces

2 teaspoons caraway seeds

¾ pound Savoy cabbage, cored and thinly sliced

1 cup water

½ teaspoon freshly ground black pepper

Grated Parmesan cheese for garnish

1. Add the grape seed oil and guanciale to a 10-inch skillet over high heat and cook until the guanciale fat has been rendered and the bits are crispy, about 2 minutes. Add the mushrooms and caraway seeds. Cook until the mushrooms release their liquid and are tender and brown, about 8 to 10 minutes. Keep stirring so that they don't stick to the bottom of the pan.

2. Bring a large pot of salted water (see page 29) to a boil.

3. Add the cabbage to the mushroom mixture in the skillet. Add the water and black pepper.

4. Add the spaghetti to the boiling water and cook until they float to the top. Cook for 2 more minutes. Use a wire-mesh skimmer or tongs to remove the spaghetti from the pot and place them directly into the skillet with the sauce. Stir to combine.

5. Serve immediately with grated Parmesan cheese.

BUCKWHEAT PAPPARDELLE, crème fraîche, fried shallots, caviar

B UCKWHEAT FLOUR IS OFTEN USED IN THE MANUFACTURE OF PASTA IN THE NORTHERN-MOST REGIONS OF ITALY, WHERE THE GRAIN GROWS IN ABUNDANCE. ITS NATURAL NUTTY FLAVOR DEMANDS, AND CAN ACCEPT, RICH SAUCES. THIS ONE IS MY TAKE ON CLASSIC BUCKWHEAT BLINI THAT ARE SERVED WITH CRÈME FRAÎCHE AND CAVIAR.

FOR THIS RECIPE I'VE USED AMERICAN SPOONBILL CAVIAR, BUT YOU CAN USE ANY SALTY, CRUNCHY FISH EGGS, FROM A JAR OF LUMPFISH CAVIAR TO SALMON ROE TO SUPERLUXURIOUS BELUGA.

WITH ITS RELATIVE EASE OF PREPARATION AND ITS SATISFYING COMBINATION OF FLAVOR AND TEXTURE, THIS PASTA IS A PERFECT ADDITION TO A SUNDAY BRUNCH.

SERVES 4–6

1 recipe Buckwheat Pasta, cut for pappardelle (pages 6 and 8)	½ cup sliced shallots	6 tablespoons caviar of your choice
¼ cup grape seed oil	8 ounces crème fraîche	

1. Add the grape seed oil and shallots to a small skillet. Turn on the heat to medium high. Cook until the shallots are golden and crispy, about 6 to 7 minutes. Place the shallots on paper towels to drain.

2. Bring a large pot of salted water (see page 29) to a boil. Add the crème fraîche and shallots to a 10-inch skillet.

3. Add the pappardelle to the boiling water and cook until they float to the top. Cook for 2 more minutes. Use a wire-mesh skimmer or tongs to remove the pappardelle from the pot and place them directly into the skillet. Stir to thoroughly coat the pappardelle with the sauce.

4. Serve immediately with a generous tablespoon of caviar over each portion.

BUCKWHEAT PAPPARDELLE, fonduta, grappa

THINKING ABOUT THE COLD WEATHER CONDITIONS IN THE PLACES WHERE BUCK-
WHEAT GROWS, ANOTHER ALPINE DISH, *FONDUTA*, CAME TO MIND. FONDUTA, THE
ITALIAN VERSION OF FONDUE, IS ENRICHED WITH A BÉCHAMEL SAUCE, MAKING IT
JUST RIGHT FOR WIDE PAPPARDELLE. THE ADDITION OF GRAPPA NOT ONLY SEEMS
TO GIVE THE IMPRESSION THAT THE SAUCE IS LIGHTER, BUT ALSO ADDS A FRUITY FLAVOR
TO THE NUTTY FONTINA CHEESE THAT GOES INTO THE FONDUTA.

YOU CAN MAKE ALL THE COMPONENTS OF THIS DISH THE MORNING BEFORE SERVING:
MAKE, ROLL, AND CUT THE PASTA. DUST IT WITH RICE FLOUR AND COVER WITH A
KITCHEN TOWEL UNTIL READY TO USE. THEN MAKE THE FONDUTA AND LET IT SIT AT
ROOM TEMPERATURE UNTIL YOU'RE READY TO EAT. LATER, WHILE THE PASTA IS COOKING,
REHEAT THE SAUCE, STIRRING CONTINUALLY TO KEEP IT FROM CURDLING.

SERVES 4–6

1 recipe Buckwheat Pasta, cut for pappardelle (pages 6 and 8)

2 cups whole milk

2 tablespoons unsalted butter

2 tablespoons all-purpose flour

1 pound fontina cheese, preferably imported Val d'Aosta, cubed

2 tablespoons grappa

1 teaspoon kosher salt

¼ teaspoon freshly ground black pepper

Grated Parmesan cheese for garnish

I. MAKE THE BÉCHAMEL: Scald the milk in a medium, nonreactive saucepan. Add the butter to a small skillet over medium-high heat. When the butter foams, add the flour. Stir together and cook until pale gold. Stir ½ cup of the scalded milk into the butter, then add all of it back into the milk. Turn the heat to medium high. Add the fontina cheese and keep stirring until it melts. Add the grappa, salt, and pepper and cook for 2 more minutes. Strain the fonduta through a sieve directly into a 10-inch skillet.

2. Bring a large pot of salted water (see page 29) to a boil. Add the pappardelle to the boiling water and cook until they float to the top. Cook for 2 more minutes. Use a wire-mesh skimmer or tongs to remove the pappardelle from the pot and place them directly into the skillet with the sauce. Stir to thoroughly coat the pappardelle with the fonduta.

3. Serve immediately with grated Parmesan cheese.

FARRO SPAGHETTI, arugula, roasted cherry tomatoes, egg yolk

WHEN COLLEEN AND I ARRIVED IN FLORENCE TO BEGIN WORK AT THE CELEBRATED RESTAURANT CIBRÈO, BENEDETTA VITALI, THE THEN WIFE OF THE OWNER, PICKED US UP AT THE TRAIN STATION. BEFORE HEADING OVER TO THE RESTAURANT, WE STOPPED FOR LUNCH AT A SMALL TRATTORIA. THE FIRST THING WE WERE SERVED WAS SPAGHETTI WITH A SPICY TOMATO SAUCE, A RAW EGG, AND LOTS OF GRATED CHEESE. THE HEAT OF THE PASTA COOKED THE EGG AND ADDED A CREAMINESS TO THE SAUCE AS WE TOSSED IT ALL TOGETHER. THIS IS MY RENDITION OF THAT DISH. THE PEPPERY ARUGULA CONTRIBUTES THE SPICE.

SERVES 4–6

1 recipe Farro Pasta, cut for spaghetti (pages 7 and 8)

2 pints cherry tomatoes, halved

2 tablespoons olive oil

1 teaspoon kosher salt

¼ teaspoon freshly ground black pepper

½ cup extra virgin olive oil

4 cups baby or coarsely chopped mature arugula leaves

4–6 organic egg yolks

Grated Parmesan cheese for garnish

1. Preheat the oven to 400°F. Add the tomatoes, olive oil, salt, and pepper to a large mixing bowl and toss to thoroughly coat the tomatoes. Place them flesh side up on a baking sheet with sides. Cook until golden and slightly crispy, abut 40 to 45 minutes.

2. Add the tomatoes, extra virgin olive oil, and arugula to another large mixing bowl. Toss to combine.

3. Bring a large pot of salted water (see page 29) to a boil. Add the spaghetti to the boiling water and cook until they float to the top. Cook for 2 more minutes. Use a wire-mesh skimmer or tongs to remove the spaghetti and place them directly into the tomato mixture. Stir to combine.

4. For each person to be served, place a portion of the spaghetti into a warm bowl. Place 1 egg yolk in the center of each portion and garnish with grated Parmesan cheese. Use a spoon and fork to toss everything together to create a creamy sauce.

5. Eat immediately!

FARRO SPAGHETTI, braised beet greens, anchovy, bread crumbs

THERE'S A CLASSIC VENETIAN PASTA DISH THAT COMBINES THE THICK TUBELIKE PASTA CALLED *BIGOLI* WITH *CIME DI RAPE* (TURNIP TOPS), ANCHOVIES, AND BREAD CRUMBS. BIGOLI ARE USUALLY MADE WITH WHOLE GRAIN FLOUR SUCH AS BUCKWHEAT, WHOLE WHEAT, OR FARRO.

INSPIRED BY THE ORIGINAL RECIPE, I USE FRESH FARRO SPAGHETTI AND THE MUCH-EASIER-TO-FIND BEET GREENS, WHICH ARE SIMILAR IN FLAVOR TO TURNIP GREENS.

SERVES 4–6

1 recipe Farro Pasta, cut for spaghetti (pages 7 and 8)

2 tablespoons grape seed oil

4 large anchovies packed in olive oil, bones removed

1 clove garlic, thinly sliced

1 pound beet greens, rinsed, tough stems removed

2 cups water

¼ teaspoon freshly ground black pepper

1 teaspoon unsalted butter

6 teaspoons toasted unseasoned bread crumbs

1. Add the grape seed oil, anchovies, and garlic to a 10-inch skillet. Turn the heat to high. When the anchovies begin to dissolve and the edges of the garlic start to turn golden, about 1 minute, add the beet greens. Toss together and cook until wilted. Add the water and cook until the greens are tender, about 10 to 12 minutes. Lower the heat and add the pepper.

2. Bring a large pot of salted water (see page 29) to a boil. Add the spaghetti to the boiling water and cook until they float to the top. Cook for 2 more minutes. Use a wire-mesh skimmer or tongs to remove the pasta from the pot and place it directly into the skillet with the sauce. Turn the heat to high. Add the butter and stir to thoroughly combine. Cook for 1 more minute.

3. Serve immediately with a bread crumb garnish.

RICOTTA CAVATELLI, mint pesto, toasted pine nuts

I N LIGURIA, A SQUIGGLY-SHAPED PASTA CALLED *TROFIE* IS OFTEN USED WITH THE REGION'S FAMOUS BASIL PESTO BECAUSE ITS TWISTED FORM ALLOWS THE PUREED HERB TO STICK IN ITS NOOKS AND CRANNIES. SIMILARLY, THE RIDGES OF THE CAVATELLI THAT I MAKE LET THIS MINT PESTO FIND SPOTS TO ADHERE TO THE PASTA.

I THINK THAT MINT IS AN UNDERUSED HERB. RATHER THAN USING IT JUST AS A GARNISH, IN THIS PESTO I'VE ALLOWED MINT'S CLEAN, PUNGENT FLAVOR TO COME INTO ITS OWN.

SERVES 4–6

1 recipe Ricotta Cavatelli (page 17)

½ cup pine nuts

1 cup extra virgin olive oil

2 cups packed fresh mint leaves

1 teaspoon kosher salt

Grated Parmesan cheese, optional garnish

1. Preheat the oven to 350°F. Place the pine nuts on a baking sheet with sides. Toast until golden brown, about 5 to 7 minutes. Let cool.

2. Add the extra virgin olive oil, mint, and cooled pine nuts to the jar of a blender and blend until the mint is smooth. There can be chunks of pine nuts in the pesto. Add the pesto and salt to a large mixing bowl and stir.

3. Bring a large pot of salted water (see page 29) to a boil. Add the cavatelli to the boiling water and cook until they float to the top. Stir a few times to keep them from sticking to the bottom of the pot. Cook for 1 more minute. Use a wire-mesh skimmer to remove the cavatelli from the pot and place them directly into the mixing bowl. Toss together to coat the cavatelli with the pesto.

4. Serve immediately with grated Parmesan cheese, if desired.

RICOTTA CAVATELLI, broccoli rabe, walnut pesto

HEN I WAS A KID, MY GRANDMOTHER USED TO MAKE CAVATELLI AND SERVE THEM WITH BROCCOLI RABE, GARLIC, AND RED PEPPER FLAKES. IN MY INTERPRETATION OF HER RECIPE, ADDING WALNUT PESTO COUNTERS THE BITTERNESS OF THE BROCCOLI RABE AND INTRODUCES SOME TEXTURE. I LIKE TO BOIL THE BROCCOLI RABE BEFORE I SAUTÉ IT IN ORDER TO TAKE OUT SOME OF THE BITTER TASTE AND TO TENDERIZE IT.

GRAZIE, NONNA.

SERVES 4–6

1 recipe Ricotta Cavatelli (page 17)

1 cup walnuts

¾ pound (1 bunch) broccoli rabe

1½ cloves garlic

½ cup plus 1 tablespoon extra virgin olive oil

½ teaspoon kosher salt

½ cup Pasta Water (page 29)

Grated pecorino Romano for garnish

1. Preheat the oven to 350°F. Place the walnuts on a baking sheet with sides. Toast until golden, about 10 minutes. Let cool.

2. Bring a large pot of salted water (see page 29) to a boil. Separate the leaves from the stalks of the broccoli rabe. Peel away the tough skin from the stalks. Add the leaves and stalks to the boiling water and cook for about 6 to 7 minutes. Drain.

3. Bring another large pot of salted water (see page 29) to a boil for the cavatelli.

4. Add the walnuts, ½ clove garlic, ½ cup of the extra virgin olive oil, and the salt to the jar of a blender and process until just before finely blended. You may want to see a few pieces of walnut.

5. Coarsely chop the broccoli rabe. Thinly slice the remaining garlic clove. Add the garlic and the remaining 1 tablespoon extra virgin olive oil to a 10-inch skillet. Turn the heat to high. When you see the edges of the garlic turn golden, about 1 minute, add the broccoli rabe and ½ cup pasta water, and sauté for 2 minutes. Turn off the heat. Use a rubber spatula to remove the walnut pesto from the blender jar. Drizzle the pesto over the broccoli rabe.

6. Add the cavatelli to the boiling water and cook until they float to the top. Cook for 1 more minute. Use a wire-mesh skimmer to remove the cavatelli from the pot and place them directly into the skillet with the sauce. Stir to combine.

7. Serve immediately with a garnish of grated pecorino Romano.

dry PASTA

From spaghetti to rigatoni, from bucatini to fusilli... for as many dry pasta shapes that exist, there are just as many sauces that can dress them. Dry pasta is the food we most associate with quick-to-make, tasty meals.

big nonna's CHICKEN RAGÙ

BIG NONNA IS WHAT I USED TO CALL MY GREAT-GRANDMOTHER. WHEN SHE WAS A GIRL, HER FAMILY KEPT CHICKENS IN THEIR BACKYARD. WHEN THE BIRDS' LAYING DAYS ENDED, THEY WERE BUTCHERED, THEN STEWED IN A TOMATO SAUCE FOR HOURS TO SOFTEN THEIR TOUGH FLESH.

YOU MIGHT THINK THAT THIS RELATIVELY THRIFTY MEAL WOULD HAVE SHOWN UP REGULARLY AT OUR FAMILY'S TABLE. IT DIDN'T. WHEN IT WAS SERVED, IT WAS A WELCOME SURPRISE. THE SAUCE WAS INVARIABLY TOSSED WITH SPAGHETTI. THE CHICKEN WAS ALWAYS REMOVED FROM THE SAUCE AND SERVED ON THE SIDE. THIS LIGHT, SUBTLE DISH IS COOKED THE DAY BEFORE IT'S SERVED SO THAT THE FLAVORS CAN FULLY DEVELOP OVERNIGHT.

SERVES 6–8

1 tablespoon grape seed oil

3½ pounds whole chicken legs, skin on

2 cloves garlic

Three 1-pound 12-ounce cans peeled whole San Marzano tomatoes, passed through a food mill

4 cups water, swirled in the tomato cans

2 teaspoons kosher salt

½ teaspoon freshly ground black pepper

1½ pounds good-quality spaghetti

Grated pecorino Romano or Parmesan cheese, optional garnish

1. Heat the grape seed oil in a large heavy-bottomed saucepan or casserole over high heat. When the oil is smoking, add the chicken skin side down and lightly brown on one side. Turn the chicken over and brown the other side. Add the garlic, pureed tomatoes, and water. Bring to a boil. Lower the heat to medium and simmer for 2 hours. Let cool. Cover and refrigerate overnight.

2. Bring the chicken and sauce to room temperature before reheating. Bring a large pot of salted water (see page 29) to a boil.

3. Turn the heat under the casserole to medium high. When the chicken is heated through, remove the chicken to a serving platter. Add the salt and pepper to the sauce.

4. Add the spaghetti to the boiling water and cook according to package directions. Use a wire-mesh skimmer or tongs to remove the spaghetti from the pot and place them directly into the sauce. Stir to combine.

5. Serve immediately with the platter of chicken on the side. Garnish with grated cheese, if desired.

nonna's SUNDAY RAGÙ

THE THOUGHT OF HAVING MY GRANDMOTHER'S SAUCE AT OUR SUNDAY LUNCHES GOT THE FAMILY THROUGH THE WEEK. LIKEWISE, IT PLEASED MY NONNA, WHO LIVED WITH HER MOTHER, BIG NONNA, TO KNOW THAT HER SAUCE BROUGHT US TOGETHER AT HER TABLE.

THE SUNDAY RAGÙ NEEDS TO BE MADE THE DAY BEFORE IT'S SERVED IN ORDER TO GIVE ITS FLAVORS TIME TO MATURE. IN SOUTHERN ITALY, THE SAUCE IS CALLED *IL RAGÙ DEL MACELLAIO*, THE BUTCHER'S RAGÙ, BECAUSE TO MAKE IT THERE'S A REQUIRED SATURDAY STOP AT THE BUTCHER'S TO PICK UP THE SMALL AMOUNTS OF A VARIETY OF MEATS THAT ARE THEN STEWED IN THE TOMATO SAUCE.

THERE ARE TWO REASONS WHY I ASK FOR CUTS OF PORK THAT COME FROM THE SHOULDER IN THIS RECIPE: FIRST, THE TOUGHER CUT OF MEAT LENDS ITSELF TO LONG COOKING; AND SECOND, IT CONTAINS THE AMOUNT OF FAT NEEDED TO BOTH RETAIN AND TRANSPORT THE FLAVOR.

SERVES 6–8

3 pounds ground pork from the shoulder

½ cup unseasoned bread crumbs

2 eggs

2 cloves garlic, minced

2 teaspoons kosher salt

½ teaspoon freshly ground black pepper

1 tablespoon grape seed oil

2 pounds pork chops from the shoulder

1 pound sweet Italian sausages

Three 1-pound 12-ounce cans peeled whole San Marzano tomatoes, passed through a food mill

4 cups water, swirled in the tomato cans

1½ pounds good-quality spaghetti

Grated pecorino Romano or Parmesan cheese, optional garnish

1. Preheat the oven to 400°F. Add the ground pork, bread crumbs, eggs, garlic, salt, and pepper to a large mixing bowl. Use your hands to roll out approximately sixteen 2-inch meatballs. Place the meatballs on a baking sheet with sides. Cook until slightly brown and firm, about 30 to 35 minutes.

2. Heat the grape seed oil in a heavy-bottomed casserole or saucepan over high heat. When the oil is smoking, brown the pork chops and sausages on all sides. Add the pureed tomatoes and water and bring to a boil. Lower the heat to medium. Add the meatballs and their pan juices and simmer for 3½ hours. Let cool. Cover and refrigerate overnight.

3. Bring the meat and sauce to room temperature before reheating. Bring a large pot of salted water (see page 29) to a boil. Turn the heat under the sauce to medium high. When the meat is heated through, remove the meat to a serving platter. Taste for seasonings and add more salt and pepper as desired.

4. Add the spaghetti to the boiling water and cook according to the package directions. Use a wire-mesh skimmer or tongs to remove the spaghetti from the pot and place them directly into the sauce. Stir to combine.

5. Serve immediately with the platter of meat on the side. Garnish with grated cheese, if desired.

nonna's holiday crab and lobster sauce, SPAGHETTI

ROM THE TIME I WAS A KID UNTIL TODAY, PART OF MY FAMILY'S CHRISTMAS RITUAL HAS BEEN THE SOUTHERN ITALIAN TRADITION KNOWN AS *SETTE PESCI*, WHERE THE MEAT-FREE CHRISTMAS EVE MEAL CONSISTS OF AT LEAST SEVEN DIFFERENT FISH DISHES. WE ATE FRIED SHRIMP, *BACCALÀ* (DRIED COD) STEWED IN TOMATO SAUCE, AND *SCUNGILLI* (CONCH) SALAD, AMONG OTHER THINGS. BUT THIS PASTA WITH CRAB AND LOBSTER WAS THE ONE DISH THAT WE LOOKED FORWARD TO MORE THAN ALL THE OTHERS. IT'S A DISH THAT OUR FAMILY MAKES FOR HOLIDAYS THROUGHOUT THE YEAR.

SERVES 6

2 tablespoons grape seed oil

3 cloves garlic, smashed

6 live blue Maryland crabs, cleaned (see Note)

¼ teaspoon red pepper flakes

Two 1-pound 12-ounce cans peeled whole San Marzano tomatoes, passed through a food mill

8 cups water

3 lobster tails

¼ cup finely chopped Preserved Lemons (page 24)

2 teaspoons kosher salt

¼ teaspoon freshly ground black pepper

1 pound good-quality spaghetti

Optional garnish: 2 tablespoons finely chopped fresh herbs, such as flat-leaf parsley, basil, or dill

1. Add the grape seed oil, garlic, and crabs to a large saucepan or stock pot over medium-high heat. Stir occasionally until the crabs turn red, about 5 minutes. Add the red pepper flakes and cook for 3 more minutes. Add the pureed tomatoes and 4 cups of the water and bring to a boil. Lower the heat to medium and simmer until reduced by half, about 2 hours. Add the lobster tails and 2 cups of the water and cook for 30 minutes. Let cool. Cover and refrigerate overnight.

2. Turn on the heat under the sauce to medium high. Add the remaining 2 cups of water and stir to combine. Cook for 10 minutes. Bring a large pot of salted water (see page 29) to a boil.

3. Remove the crab and lobster to a serving platter. Stir the lemons, salt, and pepper into the sauce.

4. Add the spaghetti to the boiling water and cook according to the package directions. Two minutes before the pasta cooking time is complete, use a wire-mesh skimmer or tongs to remove the spaghetti from the pot and place them directly into the sauce. Stir to combine.

5. Serve immediately with the platter of crabs and lobster tails on the side. Sprinkle finely chopped herbs of your choice over everything, if desired.

NOTE: *Crabs are bottom-feeders, so they need to be thoroughly cleaned before they're cooked. Soak them in generously salted water for 24 hours. When you remove them from the water, they are no longer alive. Use a stiff brush to clean between and under the legs.*

SPAGHETTI, speck, peas, cream

SPECK IS A CURED MEAT FROM THE ALTO ADIGE REGION IN NORTHERN ITALY. IN THIS SOUTHERN TYROL AREA WHERE GERMAN IS SPOKEN ON BOTH SIDES OF THE BORDER, SPECK—PORK THIGH—IS CURED LIKE PROSCIUTTO, THEN SMOKED. JUST AS I DO WITH ALL MY DISHES THAT CONTAIN PORK PRODUCTS, I LIKE TO ADD LOTS OF FRESHLY GROUND BLACK PEPPER.

WHILE IT'S OKAY TO USE FROZEN LITTLE PEAS FOR THIS RECIPE, I THINK THAT IT'S THE SWEETNESS OF FRESHLY SHELLED PEAS IN COMBINATION WITH THE SMOKY, SALTY SPECK THAT REALLY GIVES THIS DISH ITS PERSONALITY.

SERVES 4–6

1 tablespoon grape seed oil	2 cups shelled fresh or frozen little peas	½ cup Pasta Water (page 29)
½ pound speck, cut into ¼-inch dice	2 cups heavy cream	Grated Parmesan cheese for garnish
¼ teaspoon freshly ground black pepper, plus more for optional garnish	1 pound good-quality spaghetti	

1. Add the grape seed oil, speck, and the ¼ teaspoon black pepper to a 10-inch skillet. Turn on the heat to high. Cook, stirring occasionally, until the speck becomes crispy, about 4 to 5 minutes. Add the peas. Cook for 2 minutes. Add the cream and bring to a boil. Lower the heat to medium and reduce the cream by half, about 10 to 12 minutes.

2. Bring a large pot of salted water (see page 29) to a boil. Add the spaghetti to the boiling water and cook according to the package directions. Add the ½ cup pasta water to the sauce.

3. Two minutes before the pasta cooking time is complete, use a wire-mesh skimmer or tongs to remove the spaghetti from the pot and place them directly into the sauce. Stir to thoroughly coat the spaghetti with the sauce. Cook for 2 more minutes.

4. Serve immediately with the grated Parmesan cheese and, if desired, freshly ground black pepper.

SPAGHETTI, strawberries, tomato, balsamic

DURING OUR STAY IN REGGIO EMILIA, COLLEEN AND I WORKED BRIEFLY AT RISTORANTE PICCI, OWNED BY THE PICCI FAMILY, WHO ALSO PRODUCED THEIR OWN BALSAMIC VINEGAR. IT WAS AT THE RESTAURANT THAT WE DISCOVERED THE ITALIAN HABIT OF MACERATING STRAWBERRIES IN BALSAMIC VINEGAR. THE SLIGHT ACIDITY OF THE VINEGAR SERVES NOT ONLY TO EMPHASIZE THE SWEETNESS OF THE STRAWBERRIES, BUT ALSO TO ACCELERATE THE RELEASE OF THEIR JUICES. WE FOUND THIS COMBINATION VERY PLEASING.

WHEN WE OPENED OUR FIRST SFOGLIA RESTAURANT ON NANTUCKET, WE JOINED IN A LOCAL ISLAND ACTIVITY AND PICKED OUR OWN BERRIES FROM LOCAL FARMERS' STRAWBERRY FIELDS. IT WAS THEN THAT I REMEMBERED OUR ITALIAN STRAWBERRY EXPERIENCE AND ENVISIONED BALSAMIC VINEGAR—MACERATED STRAWBERRIES TOSSED WITH SOME SPAGHETTI. WHEN I TOLD COLLEEN ABOUT MY IDEA, SHE SUGGESTED THAT I ADD ACIDIC TOMATOES TO COUNTERBALANCE THE SWEET-TART STRAWBERRIES. WE HAVE CUSTOMERS WHO COME TO THE RESTAURANT ONCE A YEAR JUST FOR SPAGHETTI, STRAWBERRIES, TOMATO, BALSAMIC. IT'S BECOME ONE OF OUR SIGNATURE DISHES.

THERE IS A ONLY SMALL WINDOW BETWEEN MAY AND JUNE FOR ENJOYING THIS PASTA BECAUSE IT CAN BE MADE ONLY WITH RIPE AND IN-SEASON STRAWBERRIES.

SERVES 4–6

1 tablespoon grape seed oil

1½ cups (approximately 1 pint) fresh strawberries, large berries cut in half, small ones left whole

2 tablespoons good-quality balsamic vinegar

2 cups peeled whole San Marzano tomatoes

½ teaspoon kosher salt

¼ teaspoon freshly ground black pepper

1 pound good-quality spaghetti

1. Add the grape seed oil and strawberries to a 10-inch skillet. Turn on the heat to medium. Cook the strawberries until tender—the sides will become transparent.

2. Bring a large pot of salted water (see page 29) to a boil.

3. Stir the vinegar into the strawberries and reduce by half. The sauce will appear syrupy. Use your hands to squeeze and break up the tomatoes directly into the skillet. Add the salt and pepper and stir to combine. Lower the heat to a simmer.

4. Add the spaghetti to the boiling water and cook according to the package directions. Use a wire-mesh skimmer or tongs to remove the spaghetti from the pot and place them directly into the skillet. Stir to coat the spaghetti with the sauce.

5. Serve immediately.

LINGUINE, monkfish polpette, tomato, parsley

THIS DISH CAME OUT OF MY DREAMING ABOUT DIFFERENT WAYS OF MAKING *POL-PETTE*, OR MEATBALLS. IN THE WORDS OF RENOWNED FOOD WRITER GAEL GREENE, THESE MEATBALLS ARE "INSPIRED PARTLY BY THE ANONYMOUS FRIED FISH BALLS PEDDLED IN THE *CICCHETTI* BARS OF VENICE AND PARTLY BY HIS NOSTALGIA FOR HIS GRANDMOTHER'S SEAFOOD LINGUINE...."

MAKES 20 MONKFISH BALLS | SERVES 6–8

2 tablespoons grape seed oil

1 clove garlic, thinly sliced

⅓ cup coarsely chopped flat-leaf parsley

Two 1-pound 12-ounce cans peeled whole San Marzano tomatoes

2 cups water

FOR THE POLPETTE

1 pound monkfish, preferably cheeks

1 clove garlic, minced

2 tablespoons finely diced Preserved Lemon (page 24)

2 tablespoons coarsely chopped flat-leaf parsley

1 tablespoon coarsely chopped mint

¼ cup minced onion

1 egg

½ cup unseasoned bread crumbs

½ pound whole milk ricotta

1 teaspoon kosher salt

¼ teaspoon freshly ground black pepper

¼ teaspoon red pepper flakes

1 pound good-quality linguine

1. **MAKE THE SAUCE:** Add the grape seed oil, garlic, and parsley to a large heavy-bottomed nonreactive saucepan. Turn on the heat to medium high. Sauté for 2 minutes. Use your hands to squeeze and break up the tomatoes directly into the saucepan. Add the water and bring to a boil. Lower the heat to a simmer.

2. **MAKE THE POLPETTE:** Add the monkfish to the bowl of a food processor fitted with a metal blade and process to a paste. Add to a large mixing bowl. Add the garlic, lemon, parsley, mint, onion, egg, bread crumbs, ricotta, salt, black pepper, and red pepper flakes. Stir to thoroughly combine. Wet your hands to roll the monkfish mixture into 2-inch round balls. Drop each finished ball into the simmering sauce. Use a wooden spoon to gently stir the balls into the sauce. Place a lid askew over the saucepan. Turn up the heat to medium high and cook until the balls are firm, about 15 minutes. Lower the heat to a simmer and cook for 1½ hours. Turn off the heat. Let the sauce rest for at least 2 hours and up to 24 hours before serving (see Note).

3. Bring a large pot of salted water (see page 29) to a boil. Add the linguine to the boiling water and cook according to the package directions. Two minutes before the pasta cooking time is complete, use a wire-mesh skimmer or tongs to remove

the pasta from the pot and place it directly into the sauce. Stir to combine. Cook for 2 more minutes. Taste for seasonings and add as needed.

4. Serve immediately.

NOTE: *If the polpette have absorbed too much of the sauce, especially if they have sat overnight, revive the sauce with some Pasta Water (page 29).*

LINGUINE ALLA GENOVESE, veal ragù, salsa verde

hen Colleen and I left La Crota Ristorante, Danilo, the owner, treated us to a three-day vacation in Liguria. We were guests at a small hotel owned by a friend of his on the coast near San Remo. Each evening our host, Giorgio, fed us a different specialty of the area. Almost every dish, from salt-crusted salmon and boiled potatoes to white seafood stew to the Genovese-style veal ragù that is the base for this pasta sauce, was drizzled with pesto or *salsa verde*, green sauce. The pungent green sauces perfectly accented the other ingredients of the dishes.

Of the nine months that we spent in Italy during that sojourn, those three days in Liguria were among the most memorable.

SERVES 6

One 4- to 5-pound bone-in breast of veal, fat on

3 teaspoons kosher salt

½ teaspoon freshly ground black pepper

2 tablespoons grape seed oil

4 carrots, peeled, cut into 1-inch pieces

4 ribs celery, cut into 1-inch pieces

1 onion, cut into 1-inch pieces

Stems from 3 cups flat-leaf parsley leaves, leaves reserved for the salsa verde

1½ cups dry white wine

4 cups water, or to cover

1 cup extra virgin olive oil

3 tablespoons rinsed capers

1 large clove garlic

¼ teaspoon red pepper flakes

¼ cup fresh lemon juice

1 pound good-quality linguine

1. Preheat the oven to 400°F. Season each side of the veal breast with 1 teaspoon of the salt and ¼ teaspoon of the black pepper.

2. Heat the grape seed oil in a large heavy-bottomed, ovenproof casserole over high heat. When the oil is smoking, sear the veal on each side until golden and apparently sealed, about 6 minutes per side. When the veal is flipped over, add the carrots, celery, onion, parsley stems, and white wine. Let the wine evaporate and add the water to cover. Place the casserole in the oven and cook until the meat is falling-off-the-bone tender, about 2½ to 3 hours. Let the meat cool to the touch.

3. **MAKE THE SALSA VERDE:** Add the parsley leaves, extra virgin olive oil, capers, garlic, red pepper flakes, lemon juice, and the remaining 1 teaspoon salt to the jar of a blender and process until coarsely blended.

4. Pull the meat off the bone and add to a 10-inch skillet with the remaining cooking liquid and vegetables. Turn on the heat to medium high.

5. Bring a large pot of salted water (see page 29) to a boil. Add half the salsa verde to the skillet.

6. Add the linguine to the boiling water and cook according to the package directions. Two minutes before the pasta cooking time is complete, use a wire-mesh skimmer or tongs to remove the linguine from the pot and place them directly into the skillet. Stir to thoroughly coat the linguine with the sauce. (You may need to add ½ cup pasta water to the mixture in order to loosen the sauce.) Cook for 2 more minutes.

7. Serve immediately with a garnish of the remaining salsa verde.

SPAGHETTI, crema melanzane, ricotta salata

I LOVE THE PUREED EGGPLANT DISHES IN MIDDLE EASTERN AND INDIAN RESTAU-
RANTS. THINKING ABOUT HOW I COULD APPLY THAT KIND OF PREPARATION TO A
PASTA SAUCE, I CAME UP WITH THIS RECIPE. THE SAUCE OWES ITS SUCCESS IN NO
SMALL WAY TO THE GRATED SHARP RICOTTA SALATA AND THE FRAGRANT BASIL LEAVES
THAT PLAY WITH THE CREAMY AND TANGY EGGPLANT CREAM.

SERVES 4–6

2 medium eggplants, cut in half lengthwise, flesh side crosshatched

¾ cup olive oil

1 teaspoon kosher salt

¼ teaspoon freshly ground black pepper

1 pound good-quality spaghetti

1 clove garlic, thinly sliced

¼ teaspoon red pepper flakes

2 tablespoons Pasta Water (page 29)

¼ pound ricotta salata, grated on the large side of a box grater

6 large fresh basil leaves, thinly sliced

1. Preheat the oven to 350°F. Place the eggplants flesh side up in a baking dish. Cover with ½ cup of the olive oil, the salt, and pepper. Cook in the oven until very tender, almost collapsed, about 1 hour. Let cool.

2. Scoop out the flesh from the eggplants and put it through a food mill fitted with a fine disk. It should yield 2 cups. Scrape any excess juice from the baking dish into the pureed eggplant.

3. Bring a large pot of salted water (see page 29) to a boil. Add the spaghetti to the boiling water and cook according to the package directions. Once the pasta is in the water, begin to make the sauce.

4. Add the remaining ¼ cup olive oil, the garlic, and red pepper flakes to a 10-inch skillet over medium heat and cook until you smell the garlic cooking, 1 to 2 minutes. Stir in the pureed eggplant.

5. Two minutes before the pasta cooking time is complete, use a wire-mesh skimmer or tongs to remove the spaghetti from the pot and place them directly into the sauce. Add the 2 tablespoons pasta water and stir to combine. Cook for 2 more minutes. Add the ricotta salata and basil and stir to combine.

6. Serve immediately.

SPAGHETTI, fresh figs, hazelnuts, brown butter, basil

A t Il Poggio dei Petti Rossi, Colleen and I used to take walks after lunch while everyone else was taking a nap. Our daily routine would take us past a very ripe fig tree that was growing so close to an equally ripe walnut tree that there was a point where their branches intertwined. We would pick a fig, then crack open a walnut—the perfect treat. For us, combining figs with pasta is a natural. You must use ripe, soft figs in order for this sauce to be successful. This dish signifies the end of summer.

SERVES 4–6

1½ cups peeled hazelnuts

1 pound good-quality spaghetti

½ pound unsalted butter

6 large basil leaves, thinly sliced

1½ pounds fresh figs, stems removed, quartered

½ teaspoon kosher salt

¼ teaspoon freshly ground black pepper

½ cup Pasta Water (page 29)

Grated Parmesan cheese, optional garnish

1. Preheat the oven to 350°F. Place the hazelnuts on a baking sheet with sides. Toast until the hazelnuts are golden and the oil is extracted, about 15 minutes.

2. Add the hazelnuts to the bowl of a food processor fitted with a metal blade and process until coarsely chopped.

3. Bring a large pot of salted water (see page 29) to a boil. Add the spaghetti to the boiling water and cook according to the package directions.

4. Add the hazelnuts and butter to a 10-inch skillet. Turn on the heat to medium high. Add the basil, figs, salt, and pepper and cook, undisturbed, until tender, about 5 to 8 minutes (cooking time will depend on ripeness of the figs).

5. Two minutes before the pasta cooking time is complete, use a wire-mesh skimmer or tongs to remove the spaghetti from the pot and place them directly into the skillet. Add the ½ cup pasta water. Cook for 2 more minutes. Stir to thoroughly combine.

6. Serve immediately with grated Parmesan cheese, if desired.

SPAGHETTI, shaved melon, basil, cracked black pepper, extra virgin olive oil

IN UMBRIA, FRESH MELON IS OFTEN SERVED AT THE END OF A MIDDAY MEAL OR FOR A MIDAFTERNOON REFRESHER WITH LOTS OF FRESH LEMON JUICE, FRUITY EXTRA VIRGIN OLIVE OIL, AND CRACKED BLACK PEPPER.

AS A RESULT OF MY ENDLESS QUEST TO TURN ALL THE FOOD I LIKE INTO PASTA DISHES, I CAME UP WITH THIS PERFECT SUMMERTIME MEAL. I ADDED FRAGRANT BASIL LEAVES TO THE LUSCIOUS RIPE MELON TO PROVIDE DEPTH AND A SPLASH OF COLOR.

ALWAYS SERVE THIS DISH AT ROOM TEMPERATURE.

SERVES 4–6

1 pound good-quality spaghetti

1 ripe cantaloupe, peeled, quartered, and seeded

⅓ cup packed, thinly sliced basil leaves

1 cup fruity (from southern Italy) extra virgin olive oil

2 teaspoons kosher salt

1 tablespoon black peppercorns, smashed in a mortar with a pestle

2 tablespoons fresh lemon juice

1. Bring a large pot of salted water (see page 29) to a boil. Add the spaghetti to the boiling water and cook according to the package directions.

2. Use a mandoline to thinly julienne 1¼ pounds of the peeled, quartered, and seeded melon. Add the slices to a large mixing bowl. Add the basil, extra virgin olive oil, salt, pepper, and lemon juice to the bowl.

3. Use a wire-mesh skimmer or tongs to remove the cooked spaghetti and place them directly into the bowl with the melon. Toss to thoroughly combine.

4. Serve immediately.

SPAGHETTI AL LIMONE, almond pesto, grated ricotta salata

HEN THE ARABS INVADED SICILY, THEY BROUGHT THEIR OWN MODE OF COOKING. OVER THE YEARS, THEIR STYLE WAS INTEGRATED INTO *LA CUCINA SICILIANA*. ONE OF THE ARABS' GREATEST CONTRIBUTIONS WAS ADDING NUTS TO ALMOST EVERY DISH. THIS RECIPE COMBINES A TRADITIONAL NUT-SAUCED PASTA WITH THE SIMPLE, QUICKLY MADE, WARM-WEATHER COMBINATION OF SPAGHETTI WITH FRESH LEMON JUICE CALLED *SPAGHETTI AL LIMONE*.

SERVES 4–6

1 cup whole almonds

1 clove garlic

¾ cup extra virgin olive oil

½ teaspoon kosher salt

1 pound good-quality spaghetti

½ cup fresh lemon juice

½ cup olive oil

¾ pound ricotta salata, grated on the large side of a box grater

1. Preheat the oven to 350°F. Place the almonds on a baking sheet with sides. Toast until golden, about 12 minutes.

2. Add the toasted almonds to the bowl of a food processor fitted with a metal blade. Add the garlic, extra virgin olive oil, and salt. Process to a smooth, loose paste.

3. Bring a large pot of salted water (see page 29) to a boil. Add the spaghetti to the boiling water and cook according to the package directions.

4. Add the lemon juice and olive oil to a 10-inch nonreactive skillet. Turn on the heat to medium.

5. Two minutes before the spaghetti cooking time is complete, use a wire-mesh skimmer or tongs to remove the spaghetti from the pot and place them directly into the skillet. Stir to combine with the lemon juice and olive oil. Cook for 2 more minutes. Add three-quarters of the almond pesto and stir to combine.

6. Serve immediately with a bit of the remaining almond pesto and the grated ricotta salata.

FUSILLI al telefono

NUMBER ONE, I LOVE FUSILLI. NUMBER TWO, I LOVE THE TANGY FLAVOR OF *MOZ-ZARELLA DI BUFALA*. THIS DISH PERFECTLY MATCHES THE TWO INGREDIENTS TO MAKE A CLASSIC PASTA DISH. *AL TELEFONO* REFERS TO THE STRING OF CHEESE THAT DROPS DOWN FROM THE FUSILLI WITH EVERY FORKFUL THAT'S LIFTED OFF THE PLATE. I COULD EAT THIS DISH EVERY DAY.

SERVES 4–6

1 pound good-quality fusilli

2 tablespoons grape seed oil

1 clove garlic, thinly sliced

Two 1-pound 12-ounce cans peeled whole San Marzano tomatoes

15 large fresh basil leaves, julienned

2 teaspoons kosher salt

¼ teaspoon freshly ground black pepper

1 pound whole milk mozzarella di bufala, cut into ¼-inch pieces

Grated Parmesan cheese, optional garnish

1. Bring a large pot of salted water (see page 29) to a boil. Add the fusilli to the boiling water and cook according to the package directions.

2. Add the grape seed oil and garlic to a 10-inch skillet. Turn on the heat to high. When the edges of the garlic have turned golden, about 1 minute, use your hands to break up and squeeze the tomatoes directly into the skillet. Immediately add the basil, salt, and pepper. Bring the sauce to a boil, then lower the heat to medium.

3. When the pasta is cooked, turn off the heat under the sauce. Evenly distribute the mozzarella into the sauce. Use a wire-mesh skimmer to remove the pasta from the pot and place it directly into the skillet. Fold the fusilli into the sauce. Continue to fold until the mozzarella has melted and attached itself to the fusilli.

4. Serve immediately with grated Parmesan cheese, if desired.

PENNE, lobster, red pepper, almonds, cognac

I'VE ALWAYS BEEN DRAWN TO PASTA WITH SEAFOOD SAUCES. THIS FONDNESS MOST LIKELY STEMS FROM HAVING EATEN MY NONNA'S HOLIDAY CRAB AND LOBSTER SAUCE WITH SPAGHETTI (PAGE 64) AS A KID.

ON NANTUCKET, WE HAVE THE GOOD FORTUNE TO HAVE ACCESS TO EXCELLENT FRESH SEAFOOD. I TAKE ADVANTAGE OF ITS AVAILABILITY WHENEVER I CAN.

SERVES 4–6

¾ cup whole almonds

2 tablespoons grape seed oil

1 large red bell pepper, julienned

1 pound good-quality penne

1 pound cooked lobster meat, coarsely chopped

½ cup cognac

4 tablespoons unsalted butter

½ teaspoon kosher salt

¼ teaspoon freshly ground black pepper

⅓ cup coarsely chopped flat-leaf parsley

1. Preheat the oven to 350°F. Place the almonds on a baking sheet with sides. Toast until golden, about 12 minutes. Let cool.

2. Crush the almonds in a mortar with a pestle until coarsely chopped.

3. Add the grape seed oil and julienned pepper to a 10-inch skillet. Turn on the heat to medium high. Agitate the pan from time to time to keep the pepper strips from sticking.

4. Bring a large pot of salted water (see page 29) to a boil. Add the penne to the boiling water and cook according to the package directions.

5. Add the lobster to the skillet and stir to combine. Add the almonds and cognac. Let the cognac evaporate for 30 seconds. Add the butter, salt, and black pepper and cook until the butter has melted. Turn off the heat. Add the parsley.

6. Use a wire-mesh skimmer to remove the penne from the pot and place them directly into the skillet with the sauce. Stir to combine.

7. Serve immediately.

spiced eggplant, PENNE, white lamb ragù

LIKE THE EGGPLANT CREAM FOR THE SPAGHETTI, CREMA MELANZANE, RICOTTA SALATA (PAGE 74), THIS DISH REFLECTS MY PASSION FOR EGGPLANT PREPARED IN THE NORTH AFRICAN STYLE. AND IN MANY NORTH AFRICAN KITCHENS, EGGPLANT VERY OFTEN ACCOMPANIES LAMB. HERE, I PAIR EGGPLANT WITH LAMB RAGÙ THAT IS PREPARED *ALLA PUGLIESE*, THE WAY THEY DO IN APULIA—THAT IS, WITHOUT TOMATOES, OR *IN BIANCO*. ITS FLAVOR IS SIMILAR TO ONE OF MY FAVORITE MOROCCAN LAMB AND EGGPLANT TAGINES, OR STEWS.

YOU MIGHT CONSIDER THIS A WEEKEND OR SPECIAL-OCCASION DISH BECAUSE OF THE AMOUNT OF TIME THAT GOES INTO ITS PREPARATION.

SERVES 4–6

2 tablespoons grape seed oil	2 teaspoons red pepper flakes	8 cups 1-inch eggplant cubes
4 pounds shoulder of lamb, bone in	1 cup dry white wine	1 cup olive oil
1 onion, finely diced	6 cups water, or to cover	1 teaspoon ground cinnamon
½ cup capers	2 cups heavy cream	1 pound good-quality penne

1. Preheat the oven to 400°F. Place a heavy-bottomed ovenproof casserole over high heat. Add the grape seed oil. When it begins to smoke, add the lamb and sear on one side for 6 minutes. Turn over the lamb. Add the onion, capers, 1 teaspoon of the red pepper flakes, the white wine, and water to cover. Add the cream. Place the casserole in the oven and cook until the meat is falling-off-the-bone tender, about 3 to 3½ hours. Let cool.

2. Add the eggplant, olive oil, the remaining 1 teaspoon red pepper flakes, and the cinnamon to a large mixing bowl. Toss to coat the eggplant with the spices. Evenly distribute the eggplant on a baking sheet with sides. Cook in the 400°F oven until a finger pressed on the cubes leaves an impression, about 30 minutes.

3. Bring a large pot of salted water (see page 29) to a boil.

4. Pull the meat off the bone and add to a 10-inch skillet. Pour off the fat that will have risen to the top of the casserole, leaving the cream sauce and meat residue. Add the cream mixture to the skillet. Add the roasted eggplant. Turn on the heat to medium high.

5. Add the penne to the boiling water and cook according to the package directions. Use a wire-mesh skimmer to remove the penne from the pot and place them directly into the sauce. Stir to combine.

6. Serve immediately.

LINGUINE, calamari, salsa verde, peperoncini

THIS SIMPLE, STRAIGHTFORWARD DISH OWES ITS SUCCESS TO THE WAY THE CALA-MARI IS COOKED. COOK THE CALAMARI FOR TWO MINUTES ONLY, OR YOU WILL NEED TO COOK IT FOR AT LEAST A HALF HOUR——ANY TIME IN BETWEEN WILL RESULT IN TOUGH SQUID.

SERVES 4—6

1 pound good-quality linguine

2 tablespoons grape seed oil

1 pound calamari (squid), cut into ¼-inch rings, tentacles included

½ teaspoon red pepper flakes

Salsa verde (see page 72)

2 tablespoons fresh lemon juice

1. Bring a large pot of salted water (see page 29) to a boil. Add the linguine to the boiling water and cook according to the package directions.

2. Heat the grape seed oil in a 10-inch skillet over high heat. When the oil is smoking, add the calamari and red pepper flakes. Cook for 2 minutes, agitating the pan from time to time so that the calamari rings don't stick to the pan. Turn off the heat. Add three quarters of the salsa verde and the lemon juice.

3. Two minutes before the pasta cooking time is complete, use a wire-mesh skimmer or tongs to remove the linguine from the pot and place them directly into the skillet. Stir to combine. Turn on the heat to medium high. Cook for 2 more minutes.

4. Serve immediately with the remaining salsa verde.

SPAGHETTI alla carbonara

M Y WAY OF MAKING CARBONARA SAUCE IS AS CLOSE TO THE TRADITIONAL ITALIAN WAY AS ANY OTHER SAUCE THAT I MAKE. COAL MINERS WORKING IN THE REGION OF LAZIO, WHERE ROME IS THE CAPITAL, CREATED THIS DISH WITH INGREDIENTS THAT HELD UP DURING THE LONG HOURS SPENT IN THE MINES. LEGEND HAS IT THAT AS THEY ATE THEIR PASTA, FLECKS OF COAL WOULD DROP INTO THE DISH. THE ADDITION OF FRESHLY GROUND PEPPER REPLICATES THOSE TINY PIECES OF COAL.

SEARCH OUT ONE OF THE SAUCE'S ESSENTIAL INGREDIENTS, GUANCIALE—CURED PORK JOWL—A SPECIALTY OF CENTRAL ITALY. THE PORK JOWL IS RUBBED WITH SALT AND PEPPER, THEN CURED IN THE GROUND HIGH UP IN THE MOUNTAINS. WHILE PANCETTA, CURED PORK BELLY, MAY BE USED AS A SUBSTITUTE FOR THE GUANCIALE, YOU WILL SACRIFICE SOME OF THE AUTHENTIC FLAVOR BY USING IT.

SERVES 4–6

1 tablespoon grape seed oil

¾ cup ¼-inch diced guanciale (see Resources, page 194)

1 teaspoon freshly grated black pepper

1 pound good-quality spaghetti

1 cup Pasta Water (page 29)

6 egg yolks

1 cup grated Parmesan cheese, plus more for optional garnish

1. Bring a large pot of salted water (see page 29) to a boil.

2. Add the grape seed oil and guanciale to a 10-inch skillet. Turn on the heat to medium high. Cook until the guanciale has rendered its fat and is crispy and deep gold, about 6 to 8 minutes. Turn off the heat. Add the pepper.

3. Add the spaghetti to the boiling water and cook according to the package directions. Add the 1 cup pasta water to the guanciale.

4. Two minutes before the pasta cooking time is complete, use a wire-mesh skimmer or tongs to remove the pasta from the pot and place it directly into the skillet. Turn on the heat to medium. Add the egg yolks and stir continuously to create a creamy sauce—not scrambled eggs. If the sauce is too thick, add more pasta water. Stir in the Parmesan cheese until fully incorporated.

5. Serve immediately with more grated Parmesan cheese, if desired.

BUCATINI all'amatriciana

THE ITALIANS WOULD SAY THAT THE TRUE NAME FOR THIS DISH SHOULD BE *BUCATINI ALL'AMATRICE*, AFTER THE TOWN OF ITS ORIGIN, AMATRICE, WHICH IS NORTHEAST OF ROME. AS THE RECIPE TRAVELED FARTHER AWAY FROM THE TOWN, IT TOOK ON THE NAME BY WHICH MOST PEOPLE RECOGNIZE IT NOW, *BUCATINI ALL'AMATRICIANA*. WHATEVER IT'S CALLED, I'M DEVOTED TO ITS COMBINATION OF FLAVORS—TANGY TOMATO SAUCE THAT IS GIVEN HEFT WITH THE ADDITION OF THE SALTY, PEPPERY GUANCIALE. IT MAKES ME VERY HAPPY TO BE ABLE TO RE-CREATE A SAUCE THAT TASTES JUST LIKE MY MEMORIES OF EATING IT IN ITALY.

SERVES 4–6

1 tablespoon grape seed oil

¾ pound ¼-inch diced guanciale (see Resources, page 194)

1 medium red onion, finely diced

½ teaspoon red pepper flakes

½ cup red wine vinegar

1 pound good-quality bucatini

One 1-pound 12-ounce can peeled whole San Marzano tomatoes

1 teaspoon kosher salt

¼ teaspoon freshly ground black pepper

Grated pecorino Romano, optional garnish

1. Bring a large pot of salted water (see page 29) to a boil. Add the grape seed oil and guanciale to a 10-inch skillet. Turn on the heat to medium high. Cook until the guanciale has rendered its fat and is crispy and deep gold, about 6 to 8 minutes. Pour off all but 1 tablespoon of the fat.

2. Return the skillet to medium-high heat. Add the onion and red pepper flakes. Cook, stirring occasionally so that the onions cook evenly, until the onions are translucent and tender, about 4 to 5 minutes. Add the vinegar.

3. Add the bucatini to the boiling water and cook according to the package directions.

4. Use your hands to squeeze and break up the tomatoes directly into the skillet. Stir in the salt and black pepper.

5. Use a wire-mesh skimmer or tongs to remove the bucatini from the pot and place them directly into the skillet with the sauce. Stir to combine.

6. Serve immediately with grated pecorino Romano, if desired.

PENNE RIGATE, eggplant, oven-dried tomatoes, brodo, parsley

There was a brief period of time between my first New York City job and my move to Boston—this was before I met Colleen—when I helped a friend open a continental-style restaurant in Manhattan. My friend's background was in traditional French cooking, so when she added the obligatory pasta dish to her menu, it was sauced with vegetables cooked in a classic chicken stock. I liked the way the stock almost glazed the vegetables, so I apply that method to my own sauces from time to time. This sauce, made with simple ingredients, is immensely enriched with the addition of my full-flavored brodo.

SERVES 4–6

½ cup olive oil

2¼ cups cherry or grape tomatoes, cut in half

2 teaspoons kosher salt

¼ teaspoon freshly ground black pepper

6 cups 1-inch eggplant cubes (about 1½ medium eggplants)

5 cups Brodo (page 21)

2 cups fresh flat-leaf parsley leaves

4 tablespoons unsalted butter

1 pound good-quality penne rigate

Grated Parmesan cheese, optional garnish

1. Preheat the oven to 400°F. Drizzle a bit of olive oil on a baking sheet with sides. Place the tomatoes flesh side up on the sheet. Sprinkle 1 teaspoon of the salt and ⅛ teaspoon of the pepper over the tomatoes. Place the sheet on the top rack of the oven. Cook until the tomatoes have shriveled, about 45 minutes. Let cool.

2. Drizzle a bit of olive oil on another baking sheet with sides. Place the eggplant cubes squarely on the sheet. Pour the remaining olive oil evenly over the top. Sprinkle the remaining 1 teaspoon salt and ⅛ teaspoon pepper over the top. Place in the same oven with the tomatoes on a lower rack. Cook until tender, or until a finger pressed on the cubes leaves an impression, about 30 minutes. Let cool.

3. Bring a large pot of salted water (see page 29) to a boil.

4. Add the cooked tomatoes, eggplant, brodo, parsley, and butter to a 10-inch skillet. Turn on the heat to high. Cook until the brodo reduces by half and glazes the vegetables.

5. Add the penne rigate to the boiling water and cook according to the package directions. Two minutes before the pasta cooking time is complete, use a wire-mesh skimmer to remove the penne from the pot and place them directly into the skillet. Cook for 2 more minutes. Taste for salt and add more as needed. Stir to combine.

6. Serve immediately with grated Parmesan cheese, if desired.

FUSILLI, guanciale, carrots, vin santo, cream

M Y ORIGINAL IDEA TO PAIR CARROTS WITH GUANCIALE WAS TO MAKE A CARROT SALAD. THEN I THOUGHT ABOUT PASTA—BECAUSE PASTA IS ALWAYS THE FIRST THING I WANT TO EAT. WHAT I CAME UP WITH IS KIND OF A SPIN-OFF OF *CARBONARA* BECAUSE THE CRISPY GUANCIALE IS SERVED IN A CREAMY SAUCE THAT IS SWEETENED WITH THE FORTIFIED WINE VIN SANTO.

HERE'S WHAT FRANK BRUNI, THE NEW YORK TIMES FOOD CRITIC, HAD TO SAY ABOUT THIS PASTA IN HIS REVIEW OF OUR NEW YORK SFOGLIA: "A DISH OF PASTA THIS FANTASTIC, ITS SAUCE OF CREAM AND VIN SANTO APPLIED WITH RESTRAINT AND LEAVENED CUNNINGLY BY SHREDDED CARROT, CONVINCES A PERSON THAT WHATEVER PATH LED HIM TO IT SHOULD BE EMBRACED MORE OFTEN."

SERVES 4–6

1 tablespoon grape seed oil

½ pound diced guanciale (see Resources, page 194)

½ teaspoon freshly ground black pepper

3 medium to large carrots, peeled and finely shredded (approximately 2 cups)

½ cup vin santo or Malvasia

1 pound good-quality fusilli

1 cup heavy cream

½ cup Pasta Water (page 29)

Grated Parmesan cheese for garnish

1. Bring a large pot of salted water (see page 29) to a boil. Add the grape seed oil, guanciale, and pepper to a 10-inch skillet and turn on the heat to medium high. Cook until the guanciale has rendered its fat and is crispy and deep gold, about 6 to 8 minutes. Remove from the heat. Pour off all but ¼ cup of the fat.

2. Return the skillet to medium-high heat. Add the carrots and cook until wilted, about 2 to 3 minutes. Add the vin santo and reduce to ¼ cup.

3. Add the fusilli to the boiling water and cook according to the package directions.

4. Add the cream to the carrots and guanciale and reduce by half, about 10 to 12 minutes. Add the ½ cup pasta water to the sauce. Two minutes before the pasta cooking time is complete, use a wire-mesh skimmer to remove the fusilli from the pot and place them directly into the skillet. Toss to thoroughly coat the fusilli with the sauce. Cook for 2 more minutes.

5. Serve immediately with grated Parmesan cheese.

RIGATONI, five cheeses in parchment

COOKING FOOD IN PARCHMENT PAPER ALLOWS THE FLAVORS TO BE ABSORBED ONE INTO ANOTHER WHILE KEEPING INGREDIENTS MOIST. YOU'LL FIND VERSIONS OF PASTA COOKED IN PARCHMENT ALL OVER ITALY, FROM PALERMO UP TO MILAN.

THIS IS MY FANCY VERSION OF MACARONI AND CHEESE. THERE'S A SPECIAL SURPRISE AWAITING THE DINER WHEN THE PACKET IS OPENED.

SERVES 6

4 cups whole milk

1 pound good-quality rigatoni

3 tablespoons unsalted butter

¼ cup all-purpose flour

¾ cup cubed fontina cheese

¾ cup crumbled Gorgonzola cheese

¾ cup coarsely chopped Parmesan cheese

¾ cup cubed Montasio cheese

⅓ pound Goat's Milk Cheese (page 27)

¼ teaspoon kosher salt

⅛ teaspoon freshly ground black pepper

Six 24 by 13-inch sheets parchment paper

1. Scald the milk in a nonreactive saucepan over medium heat. Turn off the heat.

2. Bring a large pot of salted water (see page 29) to a boil. Add the rigatoni to the boiling water and cook for 6 minutes. Drain and reserve in a colander.

3. MAKE A BÉCHAMEL SAUCE: Add the butter to another nonreactive saucepan over high heat and brown. Add the flour, stirring continuously until lightly browned, about 1 minute. Add ½ cup of the already warmed milk to the flour mixture and stir to combine. Add everything back into the rest of the warm milk. Lower the heat to medium. Continue to stir until the sauce is as thick as sour cream, about 5 minutes.

4. Add the fontina, Gorgonzola, Parmesan, Montasio, and goat's milk cheeses to the béchamel. Use a whisk to thoroughly combine. It's important to stay with the sauce, continually whisking in order to achieve a thick, smooth finish—and so it won't stick to the bottom of the pan. Add the salt and pepper.

5. Return the rigatoni to the pasta pot or place it in a large mixing bowl. Strain the cheese sauce through a sieve onto the pasta. Stir to combine. Let cool.

6. Preheat the oven to 350°F. Fold each piece of parchment in half. Divide the rigatoni into 6 equal portions and place in the center of the parchment. Fold the tops of the paper over the bottoms and twist the ends to seal. Place the bundles on a baking sheet with sides. Bake until the parchment turns pale brown and you can almost see the pasta turn brownish gold through the paper, about 45 minutes.

7. Serve immediately.

RIGATONI, chick peas, rosemary, tomato

THE INGREDIENTS IN THIS DISH ARE A DEAD GIVEAWAY AS TO ITS ORIGINS. THE COMBINATION OF CHICK PEAS, TOMATOES, AND ROSEMARY TELLS YOU RIGHT AWAY THAT IT COMES FROM UMBRIA, WHERE THIS DISH WOULD PROBABLY BE MADE WITH *CICERCHIA*, AN ANCIENT LEGUME THAT RESEMBLES A GNARLY LITTLE FLATTENED CHICK PEA. HOWEVER, CICERCHIA ARE NOT AS EASY TO FIND AS CHICK PEAS.

SERVES 4–6

1 cup dried chick peas

1 large bay leaf

¼ large onion, skin on

2 sprigs fresh rosemary

½ cup dry white wine

13 cups water

1 tablespoon grape seed oil

1 garlic clove, thinly sliced

One 1-pound 12-ounce can peeled whole San Marzano tomatoes

1 pound good-quality rigatoni

½ teaspoon kosher salt

¼ teaspoon freshly ground black pepper

Grated Parmesan cheese, optional garnish

1. Add the chick peas, bay leaf, onion, 1 rosemary sprig, the white wine, and 12 cups of the water to a large saucepan. Turn on the heat to high and bring to a boil. Turn off the heat and remove the pan from the heat. Let sit for 1 hour. Return the chick pea mixture to the burner and bring to a boil. Lower the heat to medium and cook until all the water evaporates, about 1½ to 1¾ hours.

2. Bring a large pot of salted water (see page 29) to a boil.

3. Heat the grape seed oil and garlic in a 10-inch skillet over high heat. When the edges of the garlic are golden, about 1 minute, lower the heat to medium. Use your hands to squeeze and break up the tomatoes directly into the skillet. Add the chick peas, the remaining 1 cup water, and the leaves from the remaining rosemary sprig to the skillet. Stir to combine.

4. Add the rigatoni to the boiling water and cook according to the package directions. Two minutes before the pasta cooking time is complete, use a wire-mesh skimmer to remove the rigatoni from the pot and place them directly into the skillet with the sauce. Add the salt and pepper. Stir to combine. Cook for 2 more minutes.

5. Serve immediately with grated Parmesan cheese, if desired.

PENNE, umbrian lentils, pancetta

WHEN I WORKED AT IL POGGIO DEI PETTI ROSSI IN UMBRIA, I MADE THIS DISH OVER AND OVER AGAIN. THE LENTILS THAT ARE SUCH AN IMPORTANT PART OF THE SAUCE ARE FROM THE CASTELLUCCIO DI NORCIA PLAIN EAST OF THE FAMOUS ARTS-FESTIVAL TOWN OF SPOLETO. CASTELLUCCIO LENTILS ARE KNOWN ALL OVER ITALY FOR THEIR SUPERIOR FLAVOR AND EASE OF COOKING. THEY ARE SMALLER AND ROUNDER THAN THE MORE READILY AVAILABLE FLAT FRENCH LENTILS AND KEEP THEIR SHAPE AFTER THEY'VE BEEN COOKED.

I LIKE TO SERVE THIS DISH FOR VARIOUS NEW YEAR'S CELEBRATIONS BECAUSE THEIR COIN SHAPE IS SAID TO BRING PROSPERITY FOR THE COMING YEAR.

SERVES 4–6

1 cup Castelluccio lentils (see Resources, page 194)

1 large bay leaf

1 clove garlic, skin on

1 rib celery, cut into 3 pieces

1 carrot, cut into 3 pieces

3 cups water

½ cup dry white wine

1 teaspoon kosher salt

¼ pound pancetta, cut into ¼-inch dice

¼ teaspoon freshly ground black pepper

1 pound good-quality penne

Grated Parmesan cheese, optional garnish

1. Add the lentils, bay leaf, garlic, celery, carrot, water, and white wine to a large saucepan. Turn on the heat to high and bring to a boil. Turn down to a simmer and cook until the lentils are tender, about 30 minutes. Remove from the heat and add the salt. Do not stir. Let sit, undisturbed, so that the lentils absorb the remaining liquid and salt.

2. Bring a large pot of salted water (see page 29) to a boil.

3. Add the pancetta to a 10-inch skillet over medium-high heat. Cook, stirring occasionally, until crisp, about 4 to 5 minutes.

4. Remove the bay leaf, garlic, celery, and carrot from the lentils. Add the lentils, with their liquid, to the pancetta. Add the pepper and taste for salt. You may need to add more.

5. Add the penne to the boiling water and cook according to the package directions. Use a wire-mesh skimmer to remove the penne from the pot and place them directly into the skillet with the sauce. Stir to combine.

6. Serve immediately with grated Parmesan cheese, if desired.

SPAGHETTI sciuè, sciuè

SCIUÈ, SCIUÈ—PRONOUNCED, MORE OR LESS, "SHOO, SHOO,"—MEANS, QUICK, QUICK. AS A SAUCE, IT'S TYPICALLY ONE MADE WHILE THE PASTA COOKS.

THIS IS ONE OF THE FEW SAUCES THAT I START WITH EXTRA VIRGIN OLIVE OIL. I ADD IT TO A ROOM-TEMPERATURE PAN BECAUSE I DON'T WANT IT TO BURN. I WANT TO TASTE THE FULL FLAVOR OF THE OLIVE OIL.

YOU MAY HAVE NOTICED THAT MOST OF THE TIME I CALL FOR GRATED CHEESE AS AN OPTION WHEN SERVING PASTA WITH TOMATO SAUCES. MY REASONING IS THAT THE CHEESE—OR ANY DAIRY PRODUCT—IS NOT A PART OF THE ORIGINAL SAUCE FLAVORINGS. IT IS, INSTEAD, A GARNISH.

SERVES 4–6

2 tablespoons extra virgin olive oil	2 teaspoons kosher salt	Chopped flat-leaf parsley, basil, or rosemary; ground cloves; or grated Parmesan cheese for optional garnish
2 cloves garlic, thinly sliced	¼ teaspoon freshly ground black pepper	
One 1-pound 12-ounce can peeled whole San Marzano tomatoes, passed through a food mill (3 cups puree)	1 pound good-quality spaghetti	

1. Add the extra virgin olive oil and garlic to a 10-inch skillet. Turn on the heat to medium high. When the edges of the garlic turn golden, add the pureed tomatoes. Continue to cook, stirring occasionally, until reduced by half, about 10 minutes. Lower the heat. Add the salt and pepper.

2. Bring a large pot of salted water (see page 29) to a boil. Add the spaghetti to the boiling water and cook according to the package directions. Two minutes before the pasta cooking time is complete, use a wire-mesh skimmer or tongs to remove the spaghetti from the pot and place them directly into the skillet. Stir to completely coat the spaghetti with the sauce. Cook for 2 more minutes.

3. Serve immediately with one or more garnishes, if desired.

WHOLE WHEAT BIGOLI, chicken livers, escarole

THIS DISH COMBINES TWO CLASSIC VENETIAN PREPARATIONS FOR *BIGOLI*, AN EXTRUDED PASTA MADE WITH WHOLE GRAIN FLOUR. ONE, *BIGOLI IN SALSA*, IS MADE WITH ANCHOVIES, ONION, AND PARSLEY. THE OTHER, *BIGOLI CON L'ANARA* (VENETIAN DIALECT), IS COOKED IN DUCK BROTH, THEN DRESSED WITH A RAGÙ MADE WITH DUCK INNARDS. THE SUBTLE, GAMY FLAVOR OF THE CHICKEN LIVERS I USE HERE AND THE SALTY ANCHOVIES WORK WITH THE BITTER ESCAROLE TO PRODUCE A SAUCE THAT STANDS UP TO, AND COMPLEMENTS, THE HEARTY BIGOLI.

SERVES 4–6

2 tablespoons grape seed oil	6 cups packed chopped escarole	1 teaspoon kosher salt
1 clove garlic, thinly sliced	1 cup dry white wine	¼ teaspoon freshly ground black pepper
2 anchovy fillets, rinsed	1 cup water	
¾ pound chicken livers, pureed in a food processor	2 tablespoons unsalted butter	1 pound whole wheat bigoli (see Resources, page 194)

1. Add the grape seed oil and garlic to a 10-inch skillet. Turn on the heat to medium high. When the edges of the garlic have turned golden, about 1 minute, add the anchovy fillets and chicken livers. Stir to brown all sides. Add the escarole and stir to combine.

2. Bring a large pot of salted water (see page 29) to a boil.

3. Add the white wine, water, butter, salt, and pepper to the skillet. Toss to combine.

4. Add the bigoli to the boiling water and cook according to the package directions. Use a wire-mesh skimmer or tongs to remove the bigoli from the pot and place them directly into the skillet with the sauce. Stir to combine.

5. Serve immediately.

FARRO SPAGHETTI, beets, brown butter, poppy seeds

R ECIPES FROM TWO NEW YORK WOMEN RESPECTED IN THE FOOD BUSINESS INFLU-
ENCED THIS DISH: IN HER BOOK *A FRESH TASTE OF ITALY*, MICHELE SCICOLONE
(ONCE MY BROOKLYN LANDLADY) OFFERS SPAGHETTI WITH RUBIES, WHERE THE
RUBIES ARE CHUNKS OF ROASTED BEETS SAUTÉED IN OLIVE OIL, GARLIC, AND RED
PEPPER FLAKES. AT HER LEGENDARY BROOKLYN TRATTORIA AL DI LÀ, CHEF/CO-OWNER
ANNA KLINGER SERVES RAVIOLI STUFFED WITH BEETS TOSSED IN BROWN BUTTER AND
POPPY SEEDS. BEETS, TOGETHER WITH POPPY SEEDS, ARE TYPICAL IN DISHES OF THE
NORTHERN ITALIAN REGIONS OF FRIULI AND ALTO ADIGE. WITH ALL THESE FACTORS IN
MIND, I CAME UP WITH MY OWN COMBINATION OF PASTA WITH BEETS AND POPPY SEEDS.

SERVES 4–6

1 pound red beets, cleaned

¼ cup olive oil

¼ cup water

1 pound good-quality farro or whole wheat spaghetti

6 tablespoons unsalted butter

1 heaping tablespoon poppy seeds

1 teaspoon kosher salt

½ cup Pasta Water (page 29)

½ pound Goat's Milk Cheese (page 27)

1. Preheat the oven to 400°F. Place the beets in a glass or ceramic baking dish. Cover with the olive oil and water. Bake until a tester easily passes through the beets, about 1½ hours. Let cool.

2. Bring a large pot of salted water (see page 29) to a boil.

3. Peel the beets and cut into chunks. Add to the bowl of a food processor fitted with a metal blade and process to a rough puree. Add the spaghetti to the boiling water and cook according to the package directions.

4. Add the butter to a 10-inch skillet. Turn on the heat to high. Brown the butter, about 2 minutes. Add the poppy seeds and toast for 2 minutes. Add the pureed beets, salt, and the ½ cup pasta water to the skillet. Stir to fully incorporate.

5. Use a wire-mesh skimmer or tongs to remove the spaghetti from the pot and place them directly into the skillet with the sauce. Stir to combine.

6. Divide the spaghetti into equal portions and place on warm plates. Use two round or oval soupspoons to form little balls of the goat's milk cheese. Place a ball on top of each serving.

7. Serve immediately.

SPAGHETTI, fennel, artichoke ragù, dill, toasted almonds, mascarpone

WHEN COLLEEN AND I WERE VISITING HER MOTHER'S RELATIVES IN SICILY, THEY OFTEN MADE A SIMPLE DISH OF BROKEN SPAGHETTI COOKED WITH ARTICHOKES, ARTICHOKE BROTH, AND WILD FENNEL FRONDS, WHICH HAVE A DILL-LIKE FLAVOR. THE FINISHED DISH HAD ALMOST A RISOTTO QUALITY.

YOU CAN CALL THIS RECIPE A DESCENDANT OF THAT DISH. I'VE TRIED TO REPLICATE THE ORIGINAL PASTA'S FLAVOR BY USING DILL IN PLACE OF FENNEL FRONDS, THEN ACTUALLY ADDING FENNEL. I CHOSE ALMONDS FOR THEIR CRUNCH, AND BECAUSE THEY ALWAYS REMIND ME OF SICILY.

SERVES 4–6

1 cup almonds

2 tablespoons grape seed oil

1 small onion, thinly sliced

1 medium fennel bulb, cored and thinly sliced

6 baby or 3 large artichokes, prepared as on page 48

¼ cup finely chopped fresh dill

1 cup dry white wine

2 cups water

3 tablespoons unsalted butter

1 tablespoon fresh lemon juice

1 teaspoon kosher salt

¼ teaspoon freshly ground black pepper

1 pound good-quality spaghetti

6 tablespoons mascarpone

1. Preheat the oven to 350°F. Place the almonds on a baking sheet with sides. Toast until golden, about 12 minutes. Let cool. Place the almonds in the bowl of a food processor fitted with a metal blade and coarsely grind.

2. Add the grape seed oil, onion, fennel, and artichokes to a 10-inch skillet. Turn on the heat to medium high. Cook until just tender, about 4 to 5 minutes. Stir in the dill. Add the white wine and reduce by half. Add the water and cook for 30 minutes, or until the vegetables are soft.

3. Bring a large pot of salted water (see page 29) to a boil.

4. Add the butter, lemon juice, salt, and pepper to the skillet with the vegetables.

5. Add the spaghetti to the boiling water and cook according to the package directions. Two minutes before the pasta cooking time is complete, use tongs or a wire-mesh skimmer to remove the spaghetti from the pot and place them directly into the skillet with the sauce. Cook for 2 more minutes.

6. Divide the spaghetti evenly among individual plates and garnish each serving with a tablespoon of mascarpone and a generous sprinkling of ground almonds.

7. Serve immediately.

SPAGHETTI, chicken thighs, dill, lima beans

 THIS RECIPE IS A COMBINATION OF THE PREVIOUS RECIPE AND BIG NONNA'S CHICKEN RAGÙ (PAGE 61).

SERVES 4–6

2 pounds chicken thighs, skin on, bone in

2 teaspoons kosher salt

¼ teaspoon freshly ground black pepper

1 tablespoon grape seed oil

1 cup thinly sliced onions

½ cup chopped fresh dill

1 cup dry white wine

1 cup lima beans

2 cups water

1 pound good-quality spaghetti

½ cup Pasta Water (page 29)

1. Add the chicken thighs, salt, and pepper to a large mixing bowl. Toss to thoroughly coat the thighs with the seasoning.

2. Heat the grape seed oil in a 10-inch skillet over high heat. When the oil is smoking, add the thighs skin side down and cook until the skin has browned, about 6 to 8 minutes. Turn over the thighs and brown for about 3 to 4 minutes. Add the onions, dill, and white wine. Add the lima beans. Reduce the wine by half, about 5 minutes. Add the water and bring to a boil. Lower the heat to medium. Cook until the chicken is falling-off-the-bone tender, about 1¼ hours. Turn off the heat. Working within the skillet, remove the skin and bones from the chicken. Shred the meat.

3. Bring a large pot of salted water (see page 29) to a boil. Add the spaghetti to the boiling water and cook according to the package directions. Two minutes before the pasta cooking time is complete, use a wire-mesh skimmer or tongs to remove the spaghetti from the pot and place them directly into the skillet. Turn on the heat to medium high. Add the ½ cup pasta water and stir to combine the spaghetti with the sauce. Cook for 2 more minutes.

4. Serve immediately.

FREGULA RISOTTO STYLE, lobster, red pepper, lemon cream, tarragon

REGULA IS A SARDINIAN PASTA THAT IS DIRECTLY DESCENDED FROM NORTH AFRICAN COUSCOUS. ITS NAME, HOWEVER, COMES FROM THE ITALIAN VERB *FREGARE*, TO RUB. FREGULA IS MADE WITH SEMOLINA FLOUR AND LUKEWARM WATER. AFTER THE DOUGH HAS DRIED OUT, IT'S GRATED—OR RUBBED ON A GRATER—TO FORM IRREGULAR BITS.

IN SARDINIA, FREGULA IS USED IN SOUPS AND SEAFOOD STEWS THAT ARE SCENTED WITH THE SARDINIAN HERB OF CHOICE, MINT. I TOOK THE FREGULA COOKING STYLES ONE STEP FURTHER BY COOKING IT RISOTTO STYLE, ADDING LOBSTER HIGHLIGHTED WITH TARRAGON.

SERVES 4–6

1 cup heavy cream

1 lemon, cut in half

2 tablespoons grape seed oil

1/3 cup finely diced onion

3 cups fregula (see Resources, page 194)

1/2 cup dry white wine

6 cups water

2 tablespoons unsalted butter

1½ cups coarsely chopped red bell peppers

3 sprigs fresh tarragon, leaves removed

1/3 cup grated Parmesan cheese

1 teaspoon kosher salt

1/4 teaspoon freshly ground black pepper

3/4 pound lobster meat, coarsely chopped

1. Heat the cream in a nonreactive saucepan over medium heat. Add the lemon halves flesh side down. Reduce the heat to a simmer. Cook until the cream is reduced by half, about 30 minutes. Remove from the heat and let cool with the lemon. Strain the cooled lemon cream.

2. Add the grape seed oil and onion to a saucepan. Turn on the heat to medium. Cook until the onion is translucent, about 1 to 2 minutes. Add the fregula, toss to coat with the onion, and toast for 1 minute. Add the white wine. When the wine has evaporated, begin to add the water, 2 cups at a time, stirring until the water is absorbed. Keep adding the water, stirring continuously, until the pasta is tender.

3. When the last 2 cups of the water have been added, heat 1 tablespoon of the butter in a medium skillet over high heat. When it has melted, add the peppers and tarragon. Cook until the peppers are tender, about 3 to 4 minutes. Reduce the heat to low.

4. Add the remaining 1 tablespoon butter, the Parmesan cheese, salt, and black pepper to the fregula in the saucepan. Stir to combine.

5. Add the lobster and lemon cream to the peppers. Stir to combine. Cook for 1 more minute.

6. Add the hot fregula to a large serving bowl. Mound the lobster sauce in the center. It will sink into the fregula.

7. Serve immediately.

filled PASTA

I like to think about filled pastas as one-dish meals,
piatto unico. *Because I fill different kinds of pasta with
protein—fish, meat, or fowl—and then use vegetables
or herbs to sauce them, they become a complete meal.*

zucchini, mint, RAVIOLI, brown butter, poppy seeds

I LIKE TO THINK THAT THE *RAVIOLO* IS THE MAMA OF ALL THE OTHER SMALL FILLED PAS-
TAS. THESE BUNDLES OF FILLED PASTA GO BY DIFFERENT NAMES ACCORDING TO THEIR
SHAPES AND THEIR REGIONS OF ORIGIN. WHAT GOES INSIDE THEM IS ALSO REGIONAL
AND/OR SEASONAL.

IN THE SUMMERTIME, I LIKE TO TAKE ADVANTAGE OF THE GIFTS OF ZUCCHINI THAT
ARE BROUGHT TO OUR NANTUCKET RESTAURANT FROM BUMPER HARVESTS OF THE GARDENS
OF FRIENDS AND CUSTOMERS. IT'S SURPRISING HOW MUCH ZUCCHINI YOU'LL USE UP BY
MAKING THE FILLING FOR THESE RAVIOLI.

MAKES 24 RAVIOLI | SERVES 4–6

1 recipe Egg Pasta, cut into 6
sheets for filled pasta (pages 2
and 9)

2 pounds zucchini, scrubbed
clean, quartered lengthwise, and
cut into 1-inch pieces

2 tablespoons olive oil

1¾ teaspoons kosher salt

½ teaspoon freshly ground black
pepper, plus a few extra grinds

½ cup coarsely chopped fresh
mint leaves

¾ pounds whole milk ricotta

Rice flour for dusting

6 tablespoons unsalted butter

1 tablespoon poppy seeds

Grated pecorino Romano for
serving

1. Preheat the oven to 400°F. Add the zucchini, olive oil, ¼ teaspoon of the salt, and
a few grinds black pepper to a large mixing bowl. Toss together to thoroughly coat
the zucchini. Place them evenly on a baking sheet with sides. Roast until slightly
golden and soft, about 45 minutes.

2. Add the roasted zucchini to a large mixing bowl. Use the back of a wooden spoon
to smash the zucchini. Add the mint, ricotta, ½ teaspoon of the salt, and ¼ teaspoon
of the pepper. Stir to combine.

3. Cut each of the 6 pasta sheets into 3-inch squares. Line up the squares, 4 at a
time, on a clean, dry, rice flour–dusted work surface. Place 1 rounded teaspoon of
the zucchini filling in the center of each square. Use a pastry brush dipped in water
to moisten the edges of the square. Place another square turned slightly askew on
top to form an eight-pointed star. Working from the filling out to the edges, use
your fingers to press down and seal the ravioli. Store on a rice flour–dusted baking
sheet.

4. Bring a large pot of salted water (see page 29) to a boil.

5. Add the butter, the remaining 1 teaspoon salt, the remaining ¼ teaspoon pepper, and the poppy seeds to a 10-inch skillet. Turn on the heat to high and melt the butter. Turn off the heat as soon as the butter browns, about 2 minutes.

6. Use your hands to place the ravioli, 1 at a time, in the boiling water. Stir gently so that the ravioli cook evenly. After they float to the top, cook for 6 more minutes. Use a wire-mesh skimmer to remove them from the pot and place them directly into the skillet. Stir to thoroughly coat with the poppy seed butter.

7. Serve immediately with grated pecorino Romano.

CUSCINETTI, black olives, green grapes, parsley

THIS IS AN EXAMPLE OF WHY ON MY MENUS I LIKE TO USE *CUSCINETTI*, LITTLE PIL-LOWS, EVEN MORE THAN RAVIOLI. MY CUSCINETTI ALWAYS HAVE THE SAME GOAT'S MILK CHEESE–RICOTTA FILLING. THE NEUTRAL, MILDLY TANGY FILLING GIVES THEM A DELICATE FLAVOR THAT CONTRASTS WITH A VARIETY OF SAUCES.

BECAUSE GRAPES AND OLIVES GROW NEAR EACH OTHER AND ARE HARVESTED AT MORE OR LESS THE SAME TIME OF THE YEAR, I CONSIDER THEM TO BE KINDRED SPIRITS. WHEN THE BRINY OLIVES AND SWEET GRAPES GET TOGETHER AND EXCHANGE THEIR FLAVORS IN THIS SAUCE, THEY GIVE IT JUST THE KIND OF SALTY-SWEET TASTE THAT I TEND TO GO AFTER. EVEN THOUGH THE RECIPE CALLS FOR SEEDLESS GREEN GRAPES, A MORE FRAGRANT, INTENSELY FLAVORED GREEN GRAPE SUCH AS NIAGARA OR SENECA MAY WELL BE WORTH THE EFFORT TO SEED AND USE FOR THE SAUCE.

SERVES 4–6

1 recipe goat's milk–ricotta-filled Cuscinetti (page 20)

1 tablespoon grape seed oil

1 cup finely chopped red onions

1½ cups pitted black olives, such as Kalamata, coarsely chopped

1 cup seedless green grapes, cut in half

1 cup coarsely chopped flat-leaf parsley

½ cup extra virgin olive oil

½ teaspoon kosher salt

¼ teaspoon freshly ground black pepper

1. Add the grape seed oil and onions to a 10-inch skillet over medium-high heat. Cook the onions until tender, about 5 to 7 minutes. Agitate the pan from time to time to keep the onions from sticking to the bottom.

2. Add the olives, grapes, parsley, extra virgin olive oil, salt, pepper, and sautéed onions to a large mixing bowl and toss to combine. Add the pesto to a 10-inch skillet.

3. Bring a large pot of salted water (see page 29) to a boil. Add the cuscinetti to the boiling water. Stir gently so that the cuscinetti cook evenly. After they float to the top, cook for 6 more minutes. Use a wire-mesh skimmer to remove the cuscinetti from the pot and place them directly into the skillet. Carefully stir the cuscinetti into the sauce to combine.

4. Serve immediately.

CUSCINETTI, wild mushrooms, brown butter, sage

WHEN YOU'VE GOT CUSCINETTI IN THE FREEZER AND NEED TO PUT TOGETHER A SPECIAL MEAL AT THE LAST MINUTE, THIS IS THE PERFECT RECIPE TO USE. HERE YOU SAUTÉ MUSHROOMS IN BROWN BUTTER WITH FRESH SAGE, BUT YOU COULD EASILY MAKE A DELICIOUS SAUCE BY ADDING FRESH SPINACH, ASPARAGUS, OR CHOPPED NUTS TO THE BROWN BUTTER.

I HAPPEN TO LIKE CUSCINETTI COOKED AL DENTE. I LIKE THE CONTRAST OF THE SOFT FILLING WITH THE BITE OF PASTA. A COOKING TIME OF FIVE MINUTES PRODUCES AL DENTE CUSCINETTI. ADD ON ANOTHER MINUTE OR TWO FOR SOFTER PASTA, BUT BE CAREFUL NOT TO OVERCOOK, OR THE FILLING MAY SEEP OUT.

SERVES 4–6

1 recipe goat's milk–ricotta-filled Cuscinetti (page 20)

6 tablespoons unsalted butter

3 large fresh sage leaves

¾ pound (¼ pound each) mixed wild mushrooms, such as hen-of-the-woods, chanterelles, and porcini, cleaned and trimmed

1 teaspoon kosher salt

¼ teaspoon freshly ground black pepper

Grated Parmesan cheese for garnish

1. Add the butter and sage to a 10-inch skillet. Turn on the heat to high. Brown the butter and sage, about 2 minutes. Add the mushrooms, salt, and pepper and toss to coat with the butter mixture. Cook until the mushrooms' moisture is released and they become tender and brown, about 8 to 10 minutes.

2. Bring a large pot of salted water (see page 29) to a boil. Add the cuscinetti to the boiling water. Stir gently so that the cuscinetti cook evenly. After they float to the top, cook for about 5 to 6 more minutes. Use a wire-mesh skimmer to remove the cuscinetti from the pot and place them directly into the skillet with the sauce. Stir to combine.

3. Serve immediately with grated Parmesan cheese.

goat's milk cheese, spinach, CAPPELLACCI, golden raisins, saffron butter

CAPPELLACCI MEANS SHABBY HATS. WHILE CAPPELLACCI ARE A TRADITIONAL FILLED PASTA FROM EMILIA-ROMAGNA, I'VE CHOSEN TO SAUCE THESE CAPPELLACCI WITH INGREDIENTS THAT SHOW UP IN SOUTHERN ITALIAN PREPARATIONS. NOT ONLY DO I LIKE THE WAY THE MINERAL-ENRICHED SPINACH IS TEMPERED BY THE SWEET GOLDEN RAISINS, WHICH ARE THEN ENHANCED BY THE MUSTY, FRAGRANT SAFFRON BUTTER, BUT I ALSO LIKE THE COLOR COMBINATION OF THE COMPONENTS.

YOU'LL NEED BISCUIT CUTTERS TO COMPLETE THIS RECIPE.

MAKES 32 CAPPELLACCI

1 recipe Fresh Egg Pasta, cut into sheets for filled pasta (pages 2 and 9)

Rice flour for dusting

2 biscuit cutters, one 2-inch, one 2½-inch

½ pound Goat's Milk Cheese (page 27)

6 tablespoons unsalted butter

½ teaspoon saffron threads

½ cup golden raisins

¾ pound fresh spinach, tough stems removed, thoroughly rinsed and dried

½ teaspoon kosher salt

½ teaspoon freshly ground black pepper

¼ cup Pasta Water (page 29)

1. Place the pasta sheets on a clean, dry, rice flour–dusted work surface. Use the biscuit cutters to cut thirty-two 2-inch rounds and thirty-two 2½-inch rounds.

2. Fill a tipless pastry bag with a ½-inch opening with the goat's milk cheese. Line up the 2-inch rounds, 6 to 8 at a time, on the rice flour–dusted work surface. Pipe about ½ teaspoon of the filling into the center of each round. Use a pastry brush dipped in water to moisten the edges of the rounds. Place a 2½-inch round on top of each smaller one. Working from the filling out to the edges, use your fingers to press down and seal the cappellacci. Store on a rice flour–covered baking sheet.

3. Bring a large pot of salted water (see page 29) to a boil. Use your hands to place the cappellacci, 1 at a time, in the boiling water. Stir gently so that the cappellacci cook evenly. After they float to the top, cook for 6 more minutes.

4. Add the butter and saffron to a 10-inch skillet over high heat. When the butter has melted, add the raisins. Add the spinach, salt, pepper, and the ¼ cup pasta water. Cook until the spinach has wilted, about 2 to 3 minutes.

5. Use a wire-mesh skimmer to remove the cappellacci from the pot and place them directly into the skillet. Stir carefully to thoroughly coat the cappellacci with the spinach and butter.

6. Serve immediately.

TRIANGOLONI, ricotta, amaretti, radicchio, balsamic

WHEN I STARTED MY CHEF JOB AT GALLERIA ITALIANA IN BOSTON, THE KITCHEN WAS ALREADY MAKING A VERSION OF THIS TRIANGLE-SHAPED FILLED PASTA. THEY WERE FILLING THE TRIANGOLONI WITH GOAT CHEESE AND SERVING THEM WITH A SIMPLE TOMATO SAUCE. I THOUGHT THAT THEY COULD BE MORE COMPLEX, SO I ADDED SLIGHTLY SWEET, CRUSHED AMARETTI COOKIES TO THE FILLING AND TOPPED THE PASTA WITH A SWEET-AND-SOUR SAUCE OF BITTER RADICCHIO AND DENSE, SYRUPY BALSAMIC VINEGAR. WITH THIS RECIPE, I THINK THAT I'VE BROUGHT TOGETHER TWO MEMORABLE FOOD EXPERIENCES—THE RAVIOLI, FILLED WITH RADICCHIO AND BALSAMIC VINEGAR AND TOPPED WITH CRUMBLED AMARETTI AND BROWN BUTTER, FROM THE RISTORANTE PICCI IN REGGIO EMILIA; AND THE TRIANGOLONI OF GALLERIA ITALIANA.

MAKES 24 TRIANGOLONI

1 recipe Fresh Egg Pasta, cut into sheets for filled pasta (pages 2 and 9)

1 pound whole milk ricotta

8 amaretti cookies (4 double packages; see Resources, page 194), crushed

Rice flour for dusting

3 tablespoons unsalted butter

½ pound radicchio, finely shredded (about 4 cups)

¼ teaspoon freshly ground black pepper

½ cup balsamic vinegar

½ cup Pasta Water (page 29)

Grated Parmesan cheese for garnish

1. Add the ricotta and amaretti to a large mixing bowl. Stir to combine.

2. Cut 2 inches off the length of the pasta sheets and proceed to make four 4-inch squares from each sheet. Line up the squares, 4 at a time, on a clean, dry, rice flour–dusted work surface. Place 1 tablespoon of the ricotta filling slightly off center of each square. Use a pastry brush dipped in water to moisten the edges of the square. Fold the square to form a triangle. Working from the filling out to the edges, use your fingers to press down and seal the triangoloni. Trim the edges with a sharp knife. Store on a rice flour–dusted baking sheet.

3. Add the butter to a 10-inch skillet over high heat. When the butter has melted, add the radicchio and pepper. Stir to coat the radicchio with the butter.

4. Bring a large pot of salted water (see page 29) to a boil. Use your hands to place the triangoloni, 1 at a time, in the boiling water. Stir gently so that the triangoloni cook evenly. After they float to the top, cook for about 7 to 8 more minutes.

5. Stir the radicchio in the skillet. When it has wilted, add the balsamic vinegar. Agitate the pan from time to time in order to deglaze it. When the vinegar has reduced to a syrup, about 3 to 5 minutes, turn the heat to low and add the ½ cup pasta water.

6. Use a wire-mesh skimmer to remove the triangoloni from the pot and place them directly into the skillet. Gently fold into the radicchio.

7. Serve immediately with grated Parmesan cheese.

TORTELLINI in brodo

ORTELLINI ARE ANOTHER CLASSIC FILLED PASTA FROM EMILIA-ROMAGNA. THE FILLING FOR THESE LITTLE CAKES CAN BE MEAT, VEGETABLES, OR, LIKE THESE, CHEESE. TRADITIONALLY, MEAT-FILLED *TORTELLINI IN BRODO* ARE SERVED ON CHRISTMAS DAY AS THE FIRST COURSE OF THE MIDDAY MEAL. IT'S A GENTLE WAY TO BREAK THE MEATLESS RESTRICTIONS OF THE TRADITIONAL CHRISTMAS EVE MEAL.

FOR ME, THIS DISH IS AN ELIXIR, AND I LIKE IT ANYTIME. THE SIMPLE, UNCOMPLICATED FILLED PASTA COOKED IN A RICH CHICKEN BROTH (*BRODO*) HAS THE ABILITY TO BOTH COMFORT AND SOOTHE. THIS SOUP SATISFIES MY SOUL.

I ALWAYS COOK THE TORTELLINI IN WATER BEFORE I ADD THEM TO THE HOT BROTH. I DO THIS TO AVOID MAKING THE BROTH CLOUDY.

THIS RECIPE YIELDS MORE TORTELLINI THAN YOU'LL NEED FOR THE AMOUNT OF BROTH USED. I USUALLY SERVE SIX TORTELLINI PER PERSON FOR SIX SERVINGS. THE REMAINING TWENTY TORTELLINI CAN BE FROZEN (SEE NOTE).

MAKES APPROXIMATELY 56 TORTELLINI

1 recipe Fresh Egg Pasta (page 2)	2 tablespoons grated Parmesan cheese	Rice flour for dusting
¼ pound Goat's Milk Cheese (page 27)	¼ teaspoon freshly ground black pepper	1 recipe Brodo (page 21)
½ pound whole milk ricotta		

1. Add the goat's milk cheese, ricotta, Parmesan cheese, and pepper to a large mixing bowl and stir to combine. Add the filling to a tipless pastry bag with a ½-inch opening.

2. Cut each of the pasta sheets into 3-inch squares. Line up the squares at an angle, 6 to 8 at a time, on a clean, dry, rice flour–dusted work surface. Pipe about 1½ teaspoons of the filling two-thirds of the way toward one point of the square. Use a pastry brush dipped in water to moisten the edges of the pasta squares. Fold one side over the opposite side to form a triangle. Working from the filling out to the edges, use your fingers to press down and seal the tortellini. Moisten one end of the triangle. Fold one end over the other; it should look like a wonton. Store the tortellini on a rice flour–dusted baking sheet.

3. Bring a large pot of salted water (see page 29) to a boil. Add the tortellini to the boiling water. Stir gently so that the tortellini cook evenly. After they float to the top, cook for about 7 to 8 more minutes.

4. While the tortellini are cooking, heat the brodo to hot or boiling hot, depending on your preference. Use a wire-mesh skimmer to remove the tortellini from the pot and place them directly into the broth.

5. Serve immediately.

NOTE: *To freeze the tortellini for future use, place them in a single layer on a baking sheet and place in the freezer. Once frozen, they can be stored in an airtight container for up to 2 weeks. Use the tortellini not only in broth, but also with a simple tomato sauce such as Sciuè, Sciuè (page 94).*

lobster, zucchini, red pepper, LASAGNE, tarragon cream

I N ITALY AT ONE TIME, LASAGNE WAS CONSIDERED A DISH OF THE RICH. THE BAKED DISH REQUIRED AN OVEN, SOMETHING THAT COULD BE FOUND ONLY IN THE HOMES OF THE WEALTHY. IN THE TWENTIETH CENTURY, WHEN OVENS WERE A PART OF EVERY WELL-EQUIPPED KITCHEN, LASAGNE BECAME A STAPLE OF FAMILY MEALS.

IN MANY WAYS, LASAGNE IS AN ITALIAN CASSEROLE. ONCE ALL THE INGREDIENTS ARE PUT TOGETHER, YOU JUST PUT IT IN THE OVEN AND WAIT FOR IT TO COOK.

WITH THIS RECIPE, I REFER BACK TO A TIME WHEN LASAGNE WAS A WEALTHY PERSON'S DISH AND FILL IT WITH LOBSTER.

THE RECIPE FOR FRESH EGG PASTA YIELDS SIX SHEETS. YOU'LL NEED ONLY FOUR FOR THIS RECIPE (SEE NOTE).

SERVES 6–8

1 recipe Fresh Egg Pasta, cut into sheets for filled pasta (pages 2 and 9)

Olive oil

4 cups heavy cream

6 sprigs fresh tarragon plus 1 heaping tablespoon coarsely chopped leaves

2 tablespoons grape seed oil

3 cups ½-inch zucchini cubes

2 cups ¼-inch red bell pepper strips

1 teaspoon kosher salt

¼ teaspoon freshly ground black pepper

1¼ pounds lobster meat, cut into ½-inch pieces

2 pounds whole milk ricotta

¼ teaspoon red pepper flakes

1. Bring a large pot of salted water (see page 29) to a boil. Add 4 pasta sheets to the boiling water and cook for 3 minutes. Drain in a colander and drape the pasta sheets over the side. Run cool water over them to halt the cooking. Lay them flat on a clean, dry work surface and moisten each sheet with a drop of olive oil. They can be piled one on top of the other.

2. Add the cream and the tarragon sprigs to a nonreactive saucepan. Turn on the heat to medium low. Simmer until reduced by a quarter, about 15 minutes.

3. Add the grape seed oil, zucchini, red peppers, ½ teaspoon of the salt, and ⅛ teaspoon of the black pepper to a medium skillet. Turn on the heat to medium high. Cook until the zucchini are tender, about 15 minutes.

4. Add the lobster, ricotta, cooked vegetables, red pepper flakes, the chopped tarragon, and the remaining ½ teaspoon salt and ⅛ teaspoon pepper to a large mixing bowl. Stir to combine.

5. Preheat the oven to 350°F. Place 1 sheet of pasta in a 12½ by 7-inch (3-quart) baking dish. Evenly distribute ½ cup of the tarragon cream over the pasta. Evenly distribute one-third of the lobster filling over the cream. Place another sheet of lasagna on top of the lobster filling and press down firmly. Evenly distribute another third of the lobster filling over the lasagna. Cover with a third sheet of pasta. Press down firmly and evenly distribute the remaining filling. Place the last sheet of pasta over the filling. Pour ½ cup tarragon cream over the top sheet.

6. Reduce the remaining tarragon cream by half, about 7 to 8 minutes. Reserve for serving.

7. Cover the baking pan with aluminum foil. Place the baking pan on a baking sheet with sides. Bake for 1 hour. Remove the foil and bake until golden brown on top, about 20 to 30 minutes. Let rest for about 8 to 10 minutes before cutting into six to eight portions.

8. Serve with a splash of tarragon cream.

NOTE: *Cut the 2 leftover, uncooked pasta sheets into pappardelle or fettuccine (see page 8). Heavily dust the cut pasta with rice flour so the pieces won't stick together. Store in a plastic bag in the refrigerator for up to 2 days.*

ricotta, sausage, zucchini, LASAGNE, mint, parmesan

S UMMERTIME IS A GOOD TIME OF THE YEAR TO USE LASAGNE AS YOUR *PIATTO UNICO*, ONE-DISH MEAL. NOT ONLY IS LASAGNE SOMETHING THAT YOU CAN PUT TOGETHER IN THE MORNING, REFRIGERATE, AND THEN PULL OUT TO BAKE FOR DINNER, BUT DURING THE WARM WEATHER THERE'S ALSO AN ABUNDANCE AND A GREAT VARIETY OF FRESH VEGETABLES AND HERBS TO COMBINE WITH MEAT, POULTRY, OR FISH IN FILLINGS.

I HAVE A PREFERENCE FOR ZUCCHINI IN LASAGNE BECAUSE OF THE WAY ITS FLESH WITHSTANDS THE LONG COOKING PROCESS. IN THIS RECIPE, I LIKE THE SOFT, SWEET ZUCCHINI BAKED WITH THE HIGHLY FLAVORED SAUSAGE AND THE ADDED ZING OF FRESH MINT.

THE RECIPE FOR EGG PASTA YIELDS SIX SHEETS. YOU'LL NEED ONLY FOUR FOR THIS RECIPE (SEE NOTE).

SERVES 6–8

1 recipe Fresh Egg Pasta, cut into sheets for filled pasta (pages 2 and 9)

3 pounds zucchini, scrubbed clean, cut into 1-inch pieces

¼ cup grape seed oil

2 teaspoons kosher salt

½ teaspoon freshly ground black pepper

Olive oil

2 pounds whole milk ricotta

1 pound sweet Italian sausage,

casings removed, crumbled

1 cup coarsely chopped fresh mint leaves

¼ teaspoon red pepper flakes

1½ cups heavy cream

¾ cup grated Parmesan cheese

1. Preheat the oven to 350°F. Add the zucchini, grape seed oil, 1 teaspoon of the salt, and ¼ teaspoon of the black pepper to a large mixing bowl. Toss to thoroughly coat the zucchini. Spread the zucchini evenly on a baking sheet with sides. Roast until tender, about 25 to 30 minutes.

2. Bring a large pot of salted water (see page 29) to a boil. Add 4 lasagna sheets to the boiling water and cook for 3 minutes. Drain in a colander and drape the cooked noodles over the side. Run cool water over them to halt the cooking. Lay them flat on a clean, dry work surface and moisten each sheet with a drop of olive oil. They can be piled one on top of the other.

3. Add the ricotta, sausage, mint, the remaining 1 teaspoon salt, the remaining ¼ teaspoon black pepper, the red pepper flakes, and the zucchini to a large mixing bowl. Fold together to combine.

4. Cover the bottom of a 12½ by 7-inch (3-quart) baking dish with ½ cup of the heavy cream. Place 1 sheet of pasta on top. Evenly distribute half of the ricotta filling over the pasta. Sprinkle ¼ cup of the Parmesan cheese over the filling. Place another sheet of lasagna over the Parmesan and pour ½ cup heavy cream over it. Let the cream sink in before spreading the remaining filling over it. Sprinkle with another ¼ cup Parmesan cheese. Top with the last sheet of pasta. Cover with the remaining ½ cup heavy cream. Let the cream sink in. Sprinkle the remaining ¼ cup Parmesan cheese over the top.

5. Cover the baking pan with aluminum foil. Place the baking pan on a baking sheet with sides. Bake in the 350°F oven for 1 hour. Remove the foil and bake until golden brown on top, about 20 to 30 minutes. Let rest for about 8 to 10 minutes before cutting into six to eight portions.

6. Serve immediately.

NOTE: *Cut the 2 leftover, uncooked pasta sheets into pappardelle or fettuccine (see page 8). Heavily dust the cut pasta with rice flour so the pieces won't stick together. Store in a plastic bag in the refrigerator for up to 2 days.*

goat's milk cheese, pumpkin, CANNELLONI, béchamel, pumpkin seeds, bread crumbs

O N ONE OF OUR VISITS TO THE GREAT PASTA CITY OF BOLOGNA, COLLEEN AND I TOOK A CHANCE AND ATE AT A LITTLE RESTAURANT THAT WE HAD NOTICED AS WE WALKED AROUND THE CITY. WE WERE DELIGHTED WITH THE FOOD THAT WE WERE SERVED. ONE DISH THAT STAYED WITH ME WAS THE PUMPKIN-FILLED TORTELLINI SERVED FLOATING IN A DELICIOUS BROTH. I WAS SOLD ON THE COMBINATION OF PUREED PUMPKIN WRAPPED IN PASTA.

AS I VERY OFTEN HONOR THE PLACES WHERE I'VE HAD GOOD FOOD EXPERIENCES, I OFFER THIS RECIPE, CREATED FOR THE CITY OF BOLOGNA NOT ONLY BECAUSE OF ITS PUMPKIN AND PASTA COMBINATION BUT ALSO BECAUSE OF ITS CLASSIC *BESCIAMELLA*, BÉCHAMEL, WHICH IS A MUCH-USED SAUCE IN THE CITY'S *CUCINA*.

MAKES 12 CANNELLONI | SERVES 4–6

1 recipe Fresh Egg Pasta, cut into sheets for filled pasta (pages 2 and 9)

One 3-pound pumpkin, such as New England sugar pie, wrapped in aluminum foil

1 pound Goat's Milk Cheese (page 27)

1¾ teaspoons kosher salt

¾ teaspoon freshly ground black pepper

¼ teaspoon freshly ground nutmeg

¼ cup maple syrup

3 cups whole milk

1 bay leaf

3 tablespoons unsalted butter

¼ cup all-purpose flour

1 tablespoon olive oil

½ cup unseasoned bread crumbs

Grated Parmesan cheese for garnish

1. Preheat the oven to 350°F. Bake the foil-wrapped pumpkin until a tester easily passes through it, about 2¼ hours. Remove the pumpkin and lower the oven to 250°F. Let the pumpkin cool before opening it.

2. Cut open the pumpkin and scoop out the seeds. Rinse the seeds and spread them out evenly on a baking sheet with sides. Bake in the 250°F oven until brown and crispy, about 1½ hours. Remove the flesh of the pumpkin from the rind. It should yield about 2 cups (see Note) Raise the oven heat to 400°F.

3. Add the goat's milk cheese, ¾ cup of the pumpkin flesh, 1 teaspoon of the salt, ½ teaspoon of the pepper, the nutmeg, and maple syrup to a large mixing bowl. Fold together to combine.

4. Bring a large pot of salted water (see page 29) to a boil. Add the pasta sheets to the boiling water and cook for 1 minute. Plunge the pasta into a large mixing bowl filled with ice water to halt the cooking. Let cool. Lay the pasta sheets flat on a clean, dry work surface and moisten each sheet with a drop of olive oil. They can be piled one on top of the other.

5. MAKE THE BÉCHAMEL: Scald the milk and bay leaf in a nonreactive saucepan over high heat. Remove from the heat. Brown the butter with the remaining ¾ teaspoon salt and the remaining ¼ teaspoon pepper in a nonreactive saucepan over high heat. Add the flour and stir continuously until lightly browned, about 1 minute. Add ½ cup of the warm milk to the flour mixture and stir to fully incorporate. Add the mixture back into the warm milk. Turn the heat to medium and whisk until the mixture resembles sour cream.

6. Spread the olive oil in a baking dish. Cut 2 inches off the length of each pasta sheet and cut each sheet into 6 by 4-inch pieces. Line up the pasta pieces lengthwise on a clean, dry work surface. Evenly distribute ¼ cup of the goat cheese–pumpkin filling about 1 inch from the bottom of each sheet. Roll, making sure that the seams overlap. Place each roll seam side down, side by side, in two rows, in the baking dish. Pour all but 1 cup of the béchamel over the top. Combine the bread crumbs and 1 cup toasted pumpkin seeds and sprinkle over the top. Place the baking dish on a baking sheet with sides. Bake until the sides are bubbling and the top is golden brown, about 1 hour.

7. Place the cannelloni on a warm serving platter or make individual dishes for each person. Nap with the remaining béchamel.

8. Serve immediately with grated Parmesan cheese.

NOTE: *Freeze leftover pumpkin flesh in an airtight container for future use.*

crab, CANNELLONI, savory zabaglione

COLLEEN'S FATHER ALWAYS MADE CHEESE CANNELLONI COVERED WITH TOMATO SAUCE FOR HIS FAMILY'S CHRISTMAS EVE DINNERS. MY OWN FAMILY OBSERVED THE CHRISTMAS EVE TRADITION OF EATING SEVEN DIFFERENT FISH DISHES. HERE, I'VE COMBINED THESE TWO IDEAS BY STUFFING CANNELLONI WITH CRABMEAT. IT WAS COLLEEN WHO SUGGESTED THAT I MAKE A SAVORY ZABAGLIONE TO COVER THIS DISH. IT WAS A BRILLIANT IDEA BECAUSE ZABAGLIONE BAKES INTO A WONDERFULLY DENSE, CUSTARDLIKE SAUCE REMINISCENT OF MAYONNAISE.

MAKES 12 CANNELLONI | SERVES 4–6

1 recipe Fresh Egg Pasta, cut into sheets for filled pasta (pages 2 and 9)

1 tablespoon olive oil

½ pound jumbo lump crabmeat

1½ pounds whole milk ricotta

¼ teaspoon red pepper flakes

2 teaspoons kosher salt

½ teaspoon freshly ground black pepper

6 egg yolks

¼ cup dry Marsala

1 tablespoon sugar

1. Bring a large pot of salted water (see page 29) to a boil. Add the pasta sheets to the boiling water and cook for 1 minute. Plunge the pasta into a mixing bowl filled with ice water to halt the cooking. Once the pasta has cooled, rub a drop of olive oil on each sheet and pile one on top of the other on a clean, dry work surface.

2. Add the crabmeat, ricotta, red pepper flakes, 1 teaspoon of the salt, and ¼ teaspoon of the black pepper to a large mixing bowl. Fold together to combine.

3. Preheat the oven to 350°F. Spread the remaining olive oil in a baking dish. Cut 2 inches off the length of each pasta sheet and cut each sheet into 6 by 4-inch pieces. Line up the pasta pieces lengthwise on a clean, dry work surface. Evenly distribute ¼ cup of the crabmeat filling about 1 inch from the bottom of each sheet. Roll, making sure that the seams overlap. Place each roll seam side down, side by side, in two rows, in the baking dish. Place the baking dish on a baking sheet with sides.

4. MAKE THE ZABAGLIONE: Add the egg yolks, Marsala, sugar, the remaining 1 teaspoon salt, and the remaining ¼ teaspoon black pepper to the top of a double boiler. Turn on the heat to medium. When the water begins to simmer, use a whisk to beat the egg mixture continuously until it increases in volume and foams. Immediately pour the zabaglione over the top of the cannelloni. Bake until the top is golden brown and a slight crust is created, about 50 minutes to 1 hour.

5. Serve immediately.

spinach, ROTOLO, lemon cream

I WAS TRYING TO FIGURE OUT AN ALTERNATE WAY OF MAKING INDIVIDUAL PORTIONS OF LASAGNE FOR THE RESTAURANTS WHEN I CAME ACROSS A RECIPE FOR A PASTA *ROTOLO* IN ONE OF MY ITALIAN COOKBOOKS. THE ROTOLO—WHICH STARTS OUT WITH SHEETS OF PASTA SPREAD WITH A FILLING, THEN ROLLED UP LIKE A JELLY ROLL— TURNED OUT TO BE AS DIVERSE AS LASAGNE BECAUSE IT CAN BE MADE WITH A VARIETY OF INGREDIENTS. HERE'S A VERSION THAT PAIRS THE FIRST SPRINGTIME CROP OF SPINACH WITH A SIMPLE LEMON CREAM, MAKING IT A DISH PERFECTLY SUITED FOR VEGETARIANS. THE ROTOLO IS SLICED BEFORE IT'S BAKED, SO INDIVIDUAL PORTIONS ARE IN PLACE AS SOON AS THEY COME OUT OF THE OVEN.

THE RECIPE FOR FRESH EGG PASTA YIELDS SIX SHEETS. YOU'LL NEED ONLY FOUR FOR THIS RECIPE (SEE NOTE).

SERVES 6

1 recipe Fresh Egg Pasta, cut into sheets for filled pasta (pages 2 and 9)

2 lemons, cut in half

2 tablespoons grape seed oil

1 cup heavy cream

Olive oil

2 pounds fresh spinach, tough stems removed, thoroughly rinsed and steamed until wilted, about 2 minutes

½ pound whole milk ricotta

¼ teaspoon red pepper flakes

1 teaspoon kosher salt

4 teaspoons pine nuts, toasted in a 350°F oven for about 5 to 7 minutes

4 teaspoons raisins

1. Preheat the oven to 400°F. Place the lemons flesh side down in a small glass or ceramic baking dish. Coat with the grape seed oil. Roast for 30 minutes. Let cool with the juices.

2. Add the cream and the juices from the roasted lemons to a small nonreactive saucepan over medium-low heat. Simmer, stirring occasionally, until the cream is reduced by half, about 20 to 30 minutes.

3. Bring a large pot of salted water (see page 29) to a boil. Add 4 pasta sheets to the boiling water and cook for 3 minutes. Use a wire-mesh skimmer to remove them to a colander. Run cold water over the sheets to cool them. Lay them flat on a clean, dry work surface and moisten each sheet with a drop of olive oil. Pile one on top of the other.

4. Squeeze the spinach dry, coarsely chop, and place in a large mixing bowl. Add the ricotta, red pepper flakes, and salt and stir to thoroughly combine.

5. Preheat the oven to 350°F. Overlap 1 pasta sheet 4 inches over another on a clean, dry work surface. Divide the spinach filling in half. Spread one-half of the filling over three-quarters of the pasta's surface width. Sprinkle 2 teaspoons of the pine nuts and 2 teaspoons of the raisins over the spinach. Roll the sheets toward the unfilled end. Repeat with the remaining ingredients. Cut each log into 6 equal slices.

6. Cover the bottom of a rectangular baking dish with half of the lemon cream. Place the slices cut side down on the cream. Pour the remaining cream over the top. Bake until the sides are bubbling and the top is browned, about 1 hour.

7. Serve immediately.

VARIATION: *Prepare 8 artichokes as on page 48. Add the prepared artichokes with the lemon water to a nonreactive saucepan over high heat. Cook until tender, about 20 minutes. Turn off the heat and let sit in the hot water for 10 minutes. Drain the artichokes and add to the ricotta with 1 teaspoon kosher salt. Stir to combine. Spread on the pasta sheets; omit the raisins and pine nuts. Proceed with the lemon cream as directed.*

NOTE: *Cut the 2 leftover, uncooked pasta sheets into pappardelle or fettuccine (see page 8). Heavily dust the cut pasta with rice flour so the pieces won't stick together. Store in a plastic bag in the refrigerator for up to 2 days.*

rock shrimp, spinach, ROTOLO, almonds

I<small>T'S NO SECRET THAT I'M ALWAYS LOOKING FOR PLACES TO INSERT SEAFOOD INTO PASTA DISHES. FROM TIME TO TIME IN NEW YORK WE HAVE OPPORTUNITIES TO GET OUR HANDS ON SWEET, FRESH ROCK SHRIMP FLOWN UP FROM FLORIDA (SEE RESOURCES, PAGE 194). NOT ONE TO MISS AN OPPORTUNITY, I DECIDED TO FEATURE THEM IN THIS ROLLED PASTA. I ADDED THE SPINACH FOR COLOR AND, AS I DO WITH OTHER DISHES THAT HAVE CREAMY SAUCES, I ADDED TOASTED NUTS TO PROVIDE A CONTRAST AND A CRUNCH.</small>

<small>THE RECIPE FOR EGG PASTTA YIELDS SIX SHEETS. YOU'LL NEED ONLY FOUR FOR THIS RECIPE (SEE NOTE).</small>

SERVES 6

1 recipe Fresh Egg Pasta, cut into sheets for filled pasta (pages 2 and 9)

1½ cups almonds

Olive oil

1½ pounds Goat's Milk Cheese (page 27)

½ pound fresh rock shrimp or ½ pound medium-large (16–20) shrimp, peeled, deveined, and coarsely chopped

½ pound fresh spinach, tough stems removed, thoroughly rinsed and steamed until wilted, about 2 minutes

¼ teaspoon red pepper flakes

½ teaspoon kosher salt

¼ teaspoon freshly ground black pepper

1½ cups heavy cream

1. Preheat the oven to 350°F. Place the almonds on a baking sheet with sides. Toast until golden, about 16 to 18 minutes. Let cool.

2. Bring a large pot of salted water (see page 29) to a boil. Add 4 pasta sheets to the boiling water and cook for 3 minutes. Use a wire-mesh skimmer to remove them to a colander. Run cold water over the sheets to cool them. Lay them flat on a clean, dry work surface and moisten each sheet with a drop of olive oil. Pile one on top of the other.

3. Add the goat's milk cheese and shrimp to a large mixing bowl. Squeeze the spinach dry, coarsely chop, and add to the shrimp mixture. Add the red pepper flakes, salt, and black pepper.

4. Add the cooled almonds to the bowl of a food processor fitted with a metal blade and coarsely chop. Add 1 cup of the chopped almonds to the shrimp mixture. Stir to combine with the other ingredients.

5. Preheat the oven to 350°F. Overlap 1 noodle 4 inches over another on a clean, dry work surface. Divide the shrimp filling in half. Spread one-half of the filling over three-quarters of the pasta's surface width. Sprinkle ⅛ cup chopped almonds over the filling. Roll the sheets toward the unfilled end. Repeat with the remaining ingredients. Cut each log into 6 equal pieces.

6. Cover the bottom of a rectangular baking dish with ½ cup of the heavy cream. Place the slices cut side down on the cream. Pour the remaining 1 cup cream over the tops of the slices. Bake until the sides are bubbling and the top is browned, about 1 hour.

7. Serve immediately, garnished with the remaining almonds.

NOTE: *Cut the 2 leftover, uncooked pasta sheets into pappardelle or fettuccine (see page 8). Heavily dust the cut pasta with rice flour so the pieces won't stick together. Store in a plastic bag in the refrigerator for up to 2 days.*

shrimp, fave, raisins, CRESPELLE, basil

LTHOUGH THE INGREDIENTS FOR MAKING CRESPELLE AREN'T REALLY LIGHTER THAN THOSE FOR EGG PASTA, I SOMEHOW THINK OF CRESPELLE AS A MORE DELICATE HOUSING FOR THE FILLINGS. WHEN I MAKE MY FILLING AND SAUCE INGREDIENT CHOICES, I LIKE TO MIX UP FLAVOR, COLOR, AND TEXTURE. FOR THIS RECIPE, THE FAVA BEANS ADD THE TEXTURE, AND USING FRESH FAVE MAKES ALL THE DIFFERENCE. IF YOU CAN'T FIND FRESH FAVA BEANS, USE FROZEN. IF YOU CAN'T FIND THEM, THEN THE THIRD CHOICE WOULD BE LIMA BEANS—BUT ONLY AFTER A THOROUGH SEARCH FOR FAVE!

MAKES 16 CRESPELLE | SERVES 6–8

1 recipe Crespelle (page 19)	2 cups shelled and peeled fresh fava beans (see Note)	1 teaspoon kosher salt
1 pound Goat's Milk Cheese (page 27)	⅓ cup packed raisins	¼ teaspoon freshly ground black pepper
½ pound medium-large shrimp (16–20), peeled, deveined, and coarsely chopped	½ cup packed, thinly sliced fresh basil	Butter
		Extra virgin olive oil for serving

1. Add the goat's milk cheese, shrimp, fava beans, raisins, basil, salt, and pepper to a large mixing bowl. Stir together to combine.

2. Preheat the oven to 350°F. Butter a large rectangular baking dish. Line up the crespelle, 4 at a time, on a clean, dry work surface. Place ¼ cup goat's milk cheese filling along the center of each crespelle. Roll up to seal. Place 8 filled crespelle seam side down on each half of the baking dish. Bake until you can feel and see that a crust has developed, about 45 minutes.

3. Serve immediately with a drizzle of extra virgin olive oil.

NOTE: *To prepare fave for use, shell the beans. Cook them in a large pot of boiling water for 2 minutes. Immediately plunge them into a bowl of ice water to halt the cooking. Slip the skin off each bean. Now they're ready.*

chicken livers, chick peas, FAZZOLETTI, goat's milk cheese, cherry tomatoes

AZZOLETTI ARE FILLED CRESPELLE THAT ARE FOLDED TO RESEMBLE POCKET HANDKERCHIEFS.

IN MY COOKING, I LOOK FOR NEW WAYS TO PRESENT INGREDIENTS THAT ARE NOT ALWAYS WELCOME. ALTHOUGH I HAVE A GREAT LOVE FOR CHICKEN LIVERS, I REALIZE THAT MOST DINERS ARE MORE READY TO ACCEPT THEM PUREED INTO A PÂTÉ THAN ON THEIR OWN. BY PAIRING THE LIVERS WITH THE TANGY GOAT'S MILK CHEESE, THE INTENSE SWEETNESS OF ROASTED TOMATOES, AND THE CRUNCH OF CHICK PEAS, THEN FOLDING IT ALL INTO A BUTTERY CREPE, I'VE FOUND A WAY TO GET OTHERS TO ENJOY ONE OF MY FAVORITE FOODS.

MAKES 16 FAZZOLETTI | SERVES 6–8

1 recipe Crespelle (page 19)

2 pints cherry tomatoes

¼ cup olive oil

1½ teaspoons kosher salt

½ teaspoon freshly ground black pepper

1 pound Goat's Milk Cheese (page 27)

¾ pound chicken livers, coarsely chopped

1 cup drained chick peas (see page 92) or canned

Butter

Grated Parmesan cheese, optional garnish

1. Preheat the oven to 350°F. Cut the cherry tomatoes in half and add to a large mixing bowl. Add the olive oil and toss to coat the tomatoes. Place cut side up on a baking sheet with sides. Sprinkle with ½ teaspoon of the salt and ¼ teaspoon of the black pepper. Cook until the tomatoes are shriveled and slightly browned, about 1¼ hours.

2. Add the goat's milk cheese, chicken livers, chick peas, the remaining 1 teaspoon salt, and the remaining ¼ teaspoon pepper to a large mixing bowl. Stir to combine.

3. Butter a large rectangular baking dish. Line up 4 crespelle at a time on a clean, dry work surface. Place ¼ cup of the chicken liver filling in the right-hand corner of each one. Fold the crespelle in half to make a half-moon shape. Fold in half again to make a wedge shape. Place the fazzoletti at 45-degree angles in two rows in the baking dish.

4. Bake in the same oven with the cherry tomatoes until deep gold, about 45 minutes. Remove from the oven and let the tomatoes cook for 10 more minutes.

5. Serve covered with the roasted cherry tomatoes and grated Parmesan cheese, if desired.

ricotta, prunes, walnuts, FAZZOLETTI, valpolicella sauce

THIS IS PERHAPS THE ONLY STUFFED PASTA IN WHICH I USE STRAIGHT WHOLE MILK RICOTTA. I VIEW THE NEUTRAL FLAVOR OF COW'S MILK RICOTTA AS A BACKGROUND FOR THE OTHER INGREDIENTS. NEUTRAL FLAVOR IS EXACTLY WHAT'S NEEDED IN ORDER TO EMPHASIZE THE SPIRIT OF THE OTHER INGREDIENTS IN THIS DISH.

THE FILLING AND SAUCE WERE INSPIRED BY THE VALPOLICELLA WINE—SOAKED PRUNES, WHICH WERE THEN DIPPED IN CHOCOLATE, THAT COLLEEN AND I ATE WHEN WE WERE TRAVELING IN AND AROUND VERONA.

MAKES 16 FAZZOLETTI | SERVES 6–8

1 recipe Crespelle (page 19)

One 750 ml bottle Valpolicella

1 cup walnuts

1½ pounds whole milk ricotta

1 cup pitted prunes, coarsely chopped

1 teaspoon kosher salt

¼ teaspoon freshly ground black pepper

1 cup whole milk

3 teaspoons unsalted butter

1. Heat the wine in a nonreactive saucepan over medium-high heat. Reduce to ⅓ cup, about 35 minutes. It will have the consistency of maple syrup.

2. Preheat the oven to 350°F. Place the walnuts on a baking sheet with sides. Toast until golden, about 15 to 20 minutes. Let cool, then coarsely chop. Leave the oven on.

3. Add the ricotta, prunes, walnuts, salt, and pepper to a large mixing bowl. Fold together to combine.

4. Use a bit of the butter to grease a large rectangular baking dish. Line up the crespelle, 4 at a time, on a clean, dry work surface. Place ¼ cup of the ricotta filling in the right-hand corner of each one. Fold the crespelle in half to make a half-moon shape. Fold in half again to make a wedge shape. Place the fazzoletti at 45-degree angles in two rows in the baking dish. Bake for 30 minutes.

5. While the fazzoletti are baking, add the milk and butter to the reduced wine over medium heat. Cook until the butter melts. After the fazzoletti have cooked for 30 minutes, cover them with the wine sauce and cook for 15 more minutes.

6. Serve immediately.

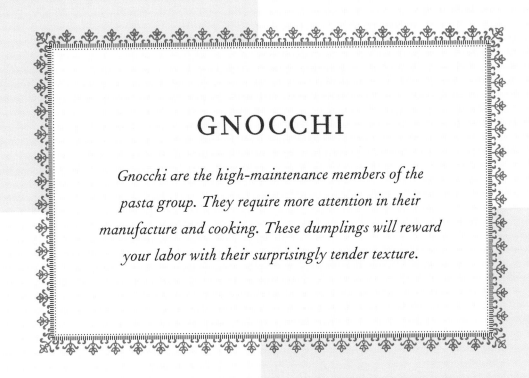

GNOCCHI

Gnocchi are the high-maintenance members of the pasta group. They require more attention in their manufacture and cooking. These dumplings will reward your labor with their surprisingly tender texture.

GNOCCHI, asparagus, toasted pistachios, mint cream

WHEN WE'RE AT HOME ON NANTUCKET, ONE OF COLLEEN'S GREAT PLEA-SURES IS TO FORAGE FOR THE WILD FRUITS AND VEGETABLES THAT GROW IN ABUNDANCE ALL OVER THE ISLAND. YEARS AGO, SHE CAME HOME WITH BUNCHES OF WHAT SHE THOUGHT WERE WILD ASPARAGUS. SHE SAUTÉED THEM AND THEN FOLDED THEM INTO A COUSCOUS SALAD. WE ATE A FEW BITES AND WERE AT FIRST PUZZLED BY THEIR BIZARRE FLAVOR. QUICKLY, HOWEVER, WE WERE OVERCOME WITH INTENSE STOMACH CRAMPS AND BEGAN TO HALLUCINATE. WE BARELY GOT OURSELVES TO THE HOSPITAL, WHERE WE WERE FORCED TO PURGE OURSELVES OF WHAT WE LATER DISCOVERED WAS BLUE INDIGO, A PLANT USED AS A NATURAL DYE, NOT ASPARAGUS.

THESE GNOCCHI, WITH THEIR THREE GREEN INGREDIENTS, ARE A TRUE CELEBRATION OF *PRIMAVERA*, WHICH LITERALLY MEANS FIRST GREEN, OR SPRINGTIME.

JUST BE CAREFUL ABOUT THE ORIGIN OF YOUR ASPARAGUS!

SERVES 4–6

1 recipe Potato Gnocchi (page 10)	1 cup fresh mint sprigs	1 teaspoon kosher salt
1 cup shelled natural pistachio nuts	½ pound thin to medium asparagus, woody parts removed, stems peeled, cut into 1-inch pieces	¼ teaspoon freshly ground black pepper
3 cups heavy cream		Grated Parmesan cheese for garnish

1. Preheat the oven to 400°F. Place the pistachios on a baking sheet with sides. Toast until golden, about 15 minutes.

2. Add the cream and mint to a nonreactive saucepan over medium-high heat. Bring to a boil, lower the heat to medium, and reduce by half, about 25 to 30 minutes.

3. Bring a large pot of salted water (see page 29) to a boil. Coarsely chop the pistachios in the bowl a food processor fitted with a metal blade or with a mortar and a pestle. Add the asparagus and pistachios to a 10-inch skillet. Strain the mint cream into the skillet. Add the salt and pepper. Turn on the heat to medium high. Cook until the asparagus are tender, about 8 to 10 minutes.

4. Add the gnocchi to the boiling water and cook until they float to the top. Cook for 1 more minute. Use a wire-mesh skimmer to remove the gnocchi from the pot and place them directly into the skillet. Carefully stir to combine with the sauce.

5. Serve immediately with grated Parmesan cheese.

GNOCCHI, duck confit, fave, mustard seed

LUCKILY FOR US, THE SEASONS FOR YOUNG, TENDER DUCK AND FAVA BEANS COINCIDE. SPRINGTIME.

WHEN I WAS A STUDENT AT THE CULINARY INSTITUTE OF AMERICA, THERE WAS A CLASS SIMPLY CALLED ESCOFFIER, WHERE WE STUDIED THE GREAT FRENCH COOKING TRADITIONS. WE OFTEN MADE DUCK CONFIT FLAVORED WITH MUSTARD SEEDS. YEARS LATER, I WAS ABLE TO APPLY THAT LESSON TO GREAT EFFECT WHEN I PUT THIS SAUCE TOGETHER.

SERVES 4–6

1 recipe Potato Gnocchi (page 10)

2¾ pounds duck legs (about 5 legs)

2 teaspoons kosher salt

½ teaspoon freshly ground black pepper

1 tablespoon grape seed oil

1 onion, sliced

4 teaspoons yellow mustard seeds

1 cup dry white wine

2 cups water

1 cup shelled and peeled fava beans (see Note, page 129)

1. Preheat the oven to 400°F. Rub the surface of the duck legs with the salt and pepper.

2. Place a heavy-bottomed ovenproof casserole over high heat. When the pan is hot, add the grape seed oil. Lower the heat to medium high. When the oil expands and covers the bottom of the pot, add the duck legs skin side down. Scatter the onion slices on top. Cook until the legs are golden brown. Turn the legs over and cook until golden brown on the other side. Add the mustard seeds and white wine. Reduce by half. Add the water. Place the casserole in the oven and cook until the duck is falling-off-the-bone tender, about 1½ to 1¾ hours. Remove from the oven and let cool.

3. Remove the meat from the bone and shred directly into the casserole. Place on the stove top and turn on the heat to medium. Add the fava beans.

4. Bring a large pot of salted water (see page 29) to a boil. Add the gnocchi to the boiling water and cook until they float to the top. Cook for 1 more minute. Use a wire-mesh skimmer to remove the gnocchi from the pot and place them directly into the casserole. Carefully stir to combine with the sauce.

5. Serve immediately.

GNOCCHI, fave, guanciale, morels

HEN I WORKED AT IL BUCO RESTAURANT IN NEW YORK, ALBERTO, ONE OF THE OWNERS, A NATIVE OF UMBRIA WITH A VERY STRONG RESPECT FOR FOOD, TAUGHT ME AN ESSENTIAL LESSON ABOUT PUTTING PASTA DISHES TOGETHER. HE TOLD ME THAT WHEN CREATING A PASTA DISH, IT'S IMPORTANT THAT ALL THE INGREDIENTS BE MORE OR LESS THE SAME SIZE SO THAT EACH FORKFUL CONTAINS SOME OF EVERYTHING.

I APPLIED ALBERTO'S IDEA WHEN MAKING THIS SAUCE WITH THE FIRST MOREL MUSHROOMS OF SPRINGTIME—WHICH I LOVE TO USE BECAUSE THEY'RE SMALL AND DON'T NEED TO BE CUT. THEIR SPONGY TEXTURE AND SUBTLE WOODSY FLAVOR WORK PERFECTLY WITH SMOKY GUANCIALE BITS AND TOOTHY FAVA BEANS.

SERVE 4–6

I recipe Potato Gnocchi (page 10)	2 cups fresh morels or 1½ cups dried morels, hydrated in 1 cup boiling water and drained	½ teaspoon kosher salt
1 tablespoon grape seed oil		½ teaspoon freshly ground black pepper
¼ pound guanciale, ¼-inch diced	2 cups shelled and peeled fava beans (see Note, page 129)	½ cup Pasta Water (page 29)
	1 tablespoon unsalted butter	Grated Parmesan cheese for garnish

1. Add the grape seed oil and guanciale to a 10-inch skillet. Turn on the heat to medium high. Cook until the fat is rendered and the guanciale is crispy, about 5 to 7 minutes.

2. Bring a large pot of salted water (see page 29) to a boil. Add the morels, fava beans, butter, salt, and pepper to the skillet. Cook, stirring occasionally.

3. Add the gnocchi to the boiling water and cook until they float to the top. Cook for 1 more minute. Add the ½ cup pasta water to the skillet. Use a wire-mesh skimmer to remove the gnocchi from the pot and place them directly into the skillet. Gently toss to combine with the sauce.

4. Serve immediately with grated Parmesan cheese.

GNOCCHI, pesto, green beans

ESTO ALLA GENOVESE IS TRADITIONALLY SERVED WITH PASTA THAT'S COATED WITH PUREED BASIL SAUCE, THEN GARNISHED WITH SLICED BOILED POTATOES AND GREEN BEANS. THE INFLUENCES FOR MY GNOCCHI WERE THIS CLASSIC RECIPE AND A DISH THAT COLLEEN AND I WERE SERVED WHEN WE WORKED IN UMBRIA. KATIA, ONE OF THE WAITERS AT IL POGGIO DEI PETTI ROSSI, INVITED US TO HER FAMILY'S HOME FOR SUNDAY LUNCH. EACH OF THE EIGHT COURSES THAT WE ENJOYED THAT DAY WAS MADE FROM INGREDIENTS THAT HAD BEEN GROWN OR RAISED ON HER FAMILY'S PROPERTY. WHAT WAS MOST MEMORABLE AMONG A LIST OF TRULY REMARKABLE FOODS WAS THE PESTO THAT DRESSED THE CAVATELLI. THE FRESHNESS WE TASTED EATING A DISH COMPRISED OF INGREDIENTS THAT WERE HARVESTED A FEW FEET FROM THE TABLE WHERE WE WERE SEATED WAS INCOMPARABLE.

SERVES 4–6

1 recipe Potato Gnocchi (page 10)

½ cup pine nuts

2 small garlic cloves

1 cup extra virgin olive oil

4 cups fresh basil leaves

1 teaspoon kosher salt

¾ pound green beans, vine end removed, cut into 1-inch pieces

Grated Parmesan cheese for garnish

1. Preheat the oven to 350°F. Place the pine nuts on a baking sheet with sides. Toast until golden, about 5 to 7 minutes.

2. Add the pine nuts, garlic, and extra virgin olive oil to the jar of a blender and process until the pine nuts are pureed, about 30 seconds. Add the basil and salt. Process until coarsely or finely chopped—your preference. Occasionally scrape the sides of the jar to ensure that all the basil is chopped. Add the pesto to a large mixing bowl.

3. Bring a large pot of salted water (see page 29) to a boil.

4. Bring a smaller pot of salted water to a boil. Add the beans and cook for about 3 to 4 minutes. Use a wire-mesh skimmer to remove them from the pot. Drain on paper towels and let cool for 1 minute. Add to the mixing bowl.

5. Add the gnocchi to the boiling water and cook until they float to the top. Cook for 1 more minute. Use a wire-mesh skimmer to remove the gnocchi from the pot and place them directly into the mixing bowl. Toss to combine.

6. Serve immediately with grated Parmesan cheese.

GNOCCHI, sweet red pepper sauce, amaretti

I MET COLLEEN WHEN WE BOTH WORKED AS LINE COOKS AT BIBA RESTAURANT IN BOSTON. SHE HAD JUST GRADUATED FROM THE CULINARY INSTITUTE OF AMERICA, AND I HAD JUST MOVED TO BOSTON FROM NEW YORK CITY. ONE OF HER FAVORITE THINGS TO MAKE WAS THE SPANISH SAUCE CALLED ROMESCO, THE DEFINING INGREDIENTS OF WHICH ARE SWEET RED PEPPERS, ALMONDS, AND BREAD. BECAUSE I LIKED THE WAY THESE INGREDIENTS PLAYED WITH ONE ANOTHER, I DECIDED TO MAKE THE TASTE COMBINATION INTO A PASTA SAUCE. I USED AMARETTI—THE COOKIES MADE WITH BITTER ALMONDS—AND ROASTED RED PEPPERS, AND INSTEAD OF USING BREAD CRUMBS, I DRAPED THE SAUCE OVER POTATO GNOCCHI.

SERVES 4–6

1 recipe Potato Gnocchi (page 10)

2 medium red bell peppers

¼ cup grape seed oil

¼ cup heavy cream

½ teaspoon kosher salt

¼ teaspoon freshly ground black pepper

6 amaretti cookies (3 double packages), crushed

1. Preheat the oven to 400°F. Place the red peppers in a glass or ceramic baking dish. Cover with the grape seed oil. Bake until the skins begin to blister, about 4 minutes. Turn the peppers over and cook until the skins have evenly blistered. Let cool.

2. Peel and seed the peppers. Add the pulp to the jar of a blender and process until smooth. Add the cream, salt, and black pepper and blend to combine.

3. Bring a large pot of salted water (see page 29) to a boil.

4. Add the pepper mixture to a 10-inch skillet. Turn on the heat to medium. Stir occasionally to prevent the sauce from sticking to the bottom.

5. Add the gnocchi to the boiling water and cook until they float to the top. Cook for 1 more minute. Use a wire-mesh skimmer to remove the gnocchi from the pot and place them directly into the skillet. Stir to combine.

6. Place the gnocchi on a warm serving platter or on individual warm plates and garnish with crushed amaretti.

7. Serve immediately.

GNOCCHI, chicken livers, hazelnuts, raisins, vin santo

I N THE CIBRÈO KITCHEN IN FLORENCE, I REPEATEDLY MADE THE FAMOUS *FEGATINI DI POLLO ALLA TOSCANA*, TUSCAN CHICKEN LIVER PÂTÉ SERVED ON CROSTINI. THE PUREED CHICKEN LIVERS WERE ALWAYS FINISHED WITH A SPLASH OF VIN SANTO AND HEAVY CREAM, WHICH SOFTENED THE ALMOST-BITTER TASTE OF THE LIVERS.

EVER SINCE THEN, I OFTEN THINK ABOUT WHAT ELSE I CAN DO WITH CHICKEN LIVERS. WITH THIS DISH, I'VE TURNED THAT UNFORGETTABLE PÂTÉ INTO A SAUCE FOR GNOCCHI.

SERVES 4–6

1 recipe Potato Gnocchi (page 10)	2 tablespoons grape seed oil	1 cup heavy cream
1 cup hazelnuts	1 garlic clove, thinly sliced	1 teaspoon kosher salt
1 cup raisins	1 pound chicken livers, medium ground in a food processor fitted with a metal blade	
½ cup vin santo or dry Marsala		

1. Preheat the oven to 350°F. Place the hazelnuts on a baking sheet with sides. Toast until golden, about 20 minutes.

2. Place the raisins in a small mixing bowl, cover with vin santo, and soak until plump.

3. Add the grape seed oil and garlic to a 10-inch skillet. Turn on the heat to medium high. Sauté until the garlic is golden around the edges, about 1 minute. Stir in the chicken liver puree and keep stirring so that it doesn't clump and keeps its "ground" appearance. Add the raisins with the vin santo, the cream, and salt. Turn down the heat to a simmer.

4. Bring a large pot of salted water (see page 29) to a boil.

5. Coarsely chop the hazelnuts and add to the chicken liver sauce.

6. Add the gnocchi to the boiling water and cook until they float to the top. Cook for 1 more minute. Use a wire-mesh skimmer to remove the gnocchi from the pot and place them directly into the sauce. Carefully stir to combine.

7. Serve immediately.

GNOCCHI, swordfish, capers

THE MOTHER OF ONE OF OUR COWORKERS AT LA CROTA RISTORANTE OWNED A SMALL BAR THAT SERVED SIMPLE FOOD. WE'D GO THERE FROM TIME TO TIME FOR LUNCH AND COULDN'T HELP BUT BE AMAZED AT THE THINGS SHE COULD PRODUCE COOKING ON JUST ONE HOT PLATE. MY FAVORITE WAS THE TROUT—OR ANY OTHER FRESHWATER FISH (PIEDMONT IS ONE OF THE FEW REGIONS OF ITALY THAT IS LANDLOCKED)—POACHED IN EXTRA VIRGIN OLIVE OIL AND CAPERS. I TOOK THAT CONCEPT AND APPLIED IT TO THE WAY I COOK THE FRESH SWORDFISH THAT SHOWS UP IN MARKETS IN THE NORTHEAST TOWARD THE END OF THE SUMMER. THE SALTY CAPERS IN COMBINATION WITH SWEET SAUTÉED ONIONS EMPHASIZE THE SALTWATER FRESHNESS OF THE FISH.

SERVES 4–6

1 recipe Potato Gnocchi (page 10)

1 cup extra virgin olive oil

1 onion, finely diced

¾ cup rinsed and drained capers

1½ pounds center-cut swordfish, dark meat removed, cut into 1-inch cubes

¼ teaspoon red pepper flakes

1 teaspoon kosher salt

2 tablespoons fresh lemon juice

1. Bring a large pot of salted water (see page 29) to a boil.

2. Add the extra virgin olive oil, onion, capers, swordfish, red pepper flakes, and salt to a skillet. Turn on the heat to medium high. Stir occasionally until the swordfish is tender, about 6 to 8 minutes. Use a wooden spoon to flake the fish while still in the skillet. Add the lemon juice and remove from the heat.

3. Add the gnocchi to the boiling water and cook until they float to the top. Cook for 1 more minute. Use a wire-mesh skimmer to remove the gnocchi from the pot and place them directly into the skillet. Stir to combine.

4. Serve immediately.

GNOCCHI, sausage, tomato, peas, smoked mozzarella

A FEW YEARS AGO, COLLEEN (PREGNANT WITH OUR SON, ROMAN); THE GIRLS, VIVIAN AND MARCELLA; AND I SPENT CHRISTMAS ON THE AEOLIAN ISLAND OF SALINA, JUST OFF THE COAST OF SICILY. ONE OF THE DISHES THAT WE WERE SERVED AT A LOCAL RESTAURANT WAS CALLED *RIGATONI ALLA FANTASIA*. THE FAT, TUBULAR PASTA WAS DRESSED WITH AN EGGPLANT PUREE, PEAS, AND SMOKED SCAMORZA —A SOFT CHEESE THAT'S SOMETHING LIKE A CROSS BETWEEN PROVOLONE CHEESE AND MOZZARELLA. I'VE ALWAYS WANTED TO USE SMOKED MOZZARELLA IN A DISH. I RECALLED THE ROMAN HABIT OF COOKING SAUSAGE WITH PEAS AND THOUGHT THOSE INGREDIENTS WOULD BE JUST THE RIGHT COMBINATION WITH SMOKED MOZZARELLA. WHEN THE SMOKY, SOFT CHEESE MELTS OVER THE GNOCCHI, SAUSAGE, AND PEAS, A *FANTASIA* IS REALIZED.

SERVES 4–6

---

1 recipe Potato Gnocchi (page 10)

1 tablespoon grape seed oil

1 pound sweet Italian sausage, casings removed

1 clove garlic, thinly sliced

2 cups peeled whole San Marzano tomatoes, crushed

1 cup water

1 cup fresh shelled or frozen peas

1 teaspoon kosher salt

¼ teaspoon freshly ground black pepper

½ pound smoked mozzarella, cut into ¼-inch cubes

---

1. Heat the grape seed oil in a 10-inch skillet over medium-high heat. When the oil is hot, add the sausage. Use a wooden spoon to break it up. Move the sausage around and cook until the pink disappears and it's browned, about 7 to 8 minutes. Add the garlic, tomatoes, water, peas, salt, and pepper.

2. Bring a large pot of salted water (see page 29) to a boil. Add the gnocchi to the boiling water and cook until they float to the top. Cook for 1 more minute.

3. While the gnocchi are cooking, evenly distribute the mozzarella over the sauce.

4. Use a wire-mesh skimmer to remove the gnocchi from the pot and place them directly into the skillet. Use a wooden spoon or spatula to carefully fold together the gnocchi and sauce.

5. Serve immediately.

GNOCCHI, sausage, cauliflower, manila clams, peperoncini

E HAVE A MUSSEL APPETIZER ON OUR RESTAURANTS' MENUS THAT'S SO POPULAR THAT WE CAN'T TAKE IT OFF, EVEN WHEN MUSSELS ARE OUT OF SEASON. FOR THOSE FEW MONTHS, WE USE MANILA CLAMS. COLLEEN HELPED ME CONCOCT THIS SUCCULENT COMBINATION OF SWEET-BRINY MUSSELS WITH SPICY SALAMI THAT IS SERVED IN A FENNEL SEED–SCENTED TOMATO BROTH.

AT CIBRÈO RESTAURANT IN FLORENCE, WE MADE A *CONTORNO*, A SIDE DISH, OF CAULIFLOWER BRAISED WITH TOMATOES, LITTLE BITS OF SALAMI, FENNEL SEEDS, AND BLACK OLIVES. IT'S OBVIOUS THAT THIS DISH IS AN OFFSHOOT OF OUR APPETIZER AND CIBRÈO'S SIDE DISH.

SERVES 4–6

1 recipe Potato Gnocchi (page 10)

1 tablespoon grape seed oil

1 clove garlic, thinly sliced

½ pound sweet Italian sausage, casings removed

4 cups small cauliflower florets

1 cup Pasta Water (page 29)

¼ teaspoon red pepper flakes

1½ cups shelled Manila clams, with their liquor

½ cup dry white wine

⅓ cup coarsely chopped flat-leaf parsley

1. Bring a large pot of salted water (see page 29) to a boil.

2. Add the grape seed oil and garlic to a 10-inch skillet. Turn on the heat to high. When the oil is hot, add the sausage. Use a wooden spoon to break up the sausage so it can render its fat. Move the sausage around and cook until the pink disappears and it's browned, about 7 to 8 minutes. Add the cauliflower and the 1 cup pasta water. Let cook until the cauliflower is tender, or until the liquid is absorbed, about 6 to 7 minutes. Add the red pepper flakes, clams with their liquor, and white wine.

3. Add the gnocchi to the boiling water and cook until they float to the top. Cook for 1 more minute. Use a wire-mesh skimmer to remove the gnocchi from the pot and place them directly into the skillet. Carefully stir to combine.

4. Serve immediately garnished with the chopped parsley.

GNOCCHI, chestnuts, porcini, sage

THERE'S NO DOUBT THAT THIS SAUCE WAS INFLUENCED BY OUR STAY IN AND AROUND ALBA, WHERE NOT ONLY WERE WHOLE CHESTNUTS A PREVALENT INGREDIENT, BUT SO WERE DISHES MADE WITH CHESTNUT FLOUR, LIKE CAKES AND GNOCCHI. I WASN'T SO CRAZY ABOUT THE GNOCCHI MADE WITH CHESTNUT FLOUR—I FOUND THEM TOO GRITTY. TO HONOR MY PIEDMONTESE CHESTNUT MEMORY, I CHOSE INSTEAD TO MAKE A SAUCE FOR POTATO GNOCCHI, USING NATURALLY SWEET, PUREED CHESTNUTS AND ANOTHER LOCAL-TO-ALBA INGREDIENT, EARTHY PORCINI MUSHROOMS. ADDING HEAVY CREAM DOES WONDERS TO MARRY THE TWO FLAVORS.

IT'S IMPORTANT TO PEEL THE SKIN FROM THE CHESTNUTS WHILE THEY'RE STILL WARM. AS SOON AS THEY COOL DOWN, THE SKIN ADHERES TO THE NUTS.

SERVES 4–6

1 recipe Potato Gnocchi (page 10)

1½ cups chestnuts

6 cups water

1 cup dried porcini mushrooms, hydrated in 2 cups boiling water, drained, and squeezed dry

10 large fresh sage leaves, thinly sliced

1 cup heavy cream

½ teaspoon kosher salt

¼ teaspoon freshly ground black pepper

½ cup Pasta Water (page 29)

Grated Parmesan cheese for garnish

1. Preheat the oven to 350°F. Use a sharp paring knife to score the flat side of the chestnuts with an X. Add the chestnuts to a saucepan and cover with 4 cups of the water. Bring to a boil. Cook for 10 minutes. Strain. Place the chestnuts on a baking sheet with sides. Bake for 30 minutes. Let cool to the touch—but they need to be warm in order to successfully peel away the shells and skins.

2. Bring a large pot of salted water (see page 29) to a boil.

3. Add the peeled chestnuts and drained porcini to the jar of a blender and process until the chestnuts are coarsely chopped. Add the blended chestnuts and porcini to a 10-inch skillet. Add the sage, cream, salt, and pepper. Turn on the heat to medium high. Cook, stirring occasionally.

4. Add the gnocchi to the boiling water and cook until they float to the top. Cook for 1 more minute. Use a wire-mesh skimmer to remove the gnocchi from the pot and place them directly into the skillet. Add the ½ cup pasta water. Stir to combine.

5. Serve immediately with grated Parmesan cheese.

GNOCCHI, braised oxtail, ginger, cocoa

ECAUSE BRAISED OXTAIL SHREDS SO EASILY, IT IS VERY OFTEN USED IN ITALY TO FILL PASTA LIKE RAVIOLI. THE COMBINATION OF COCOA POWDER AND OXTAIL GOES BACK TO THE RENAISSANCE TABLE, WHEN COCOA, LIKE ANCHOVIES, WAS USED TO INTENSIFY THE FLAVOR OF OTHER INGREDIENTS. THE SPARKLING PRESENCE OF GINGER HELPS TO MAKE THIS DISH AN ELEGANT VERSION OF MEAT AND POTATOES.

SERVES 4–6

1 recipe Potato Gnocchi (page 10)

2 pounds oxtails

2 teaspoons kosher salt

½ teaspoon freshly ground black pepper

2 tablespoons grape seed oil

1 cup thinly sliced onions

One 4-inch piece ginger, skin on, cut into 3 pieces

1 cup dry white wine

4 cups water

½ cup good-quality cocoa powder

1 tablespoon unsalted butter

½ cup whole milk

1. Preheat the oven to 350°F. Season the oxtails with 1 teaspoon of the salt and ¼ teaspoon of the pepper.

2. Heat the grape seed oil in a heavy-bottomed ovenproof casserole over high heat. When the oil is smoking, place the oxtails bone side down in the pan. Cover with the onions. Brown the oxtails on all sides. Add the ginger, white wine, and water. Sprinkle the cocoa powder over everything and carefully stir into the liquid. Bring to a boil. Place the casserole in the oven and cook until the meat is falling-off-the-bone tender and the sauce has thickened, about 2 to 2¼ hours. Let cool.

3. Bring a large pot of salted water (see page 29) to a boil.

4. Shred the meat from the bones directly back into the sauce. Remove the ginger. Place the casserole over medium-high heat. Add the butter, milk, the remaining 1 teaspoon salt, and the remaining ¼ teaspoon pepper.

5. Add the gnocchi to the boiling water and cook until they float to the top. Cook for 1 more minute. Use a wire-mesh skimmer to remove the gnocchi from the pot and place them directly into the oxtail sauce. Carefully stir into the sauce.

6. Serve immediately.

spinach, GOAT'S MILK CHEESE GNUDI, nutmeg, brown butter

NUDI ORIGINATED IN TUSCANY, WHERE PASTA DISHES AREN'T AS COMMON AS THEY ARE IN THE REST OF ITALY. THEY ARE, LITERALLY, RAVIOLI WITHOUT THE PASTA—THEY'RE NUDE! FOR CLASSIC GNUDI, YOU MAKE A SPINACH-AND-RICOTTA RAVIOLI FILLING AND BIND IT WITH AN EGG AND BREAD CRUMBS SO THE GNUDI WILL STAND ON THEIR OWN WHEN THEY'RE POACHED.

I LIKE TO USE OUR OWN GOAT'S MILK CHEESE INSTEAD OF RICOTTA FOR MY GNUDI BECAUSE I LIKE ITS SHARP FLAVOR.

SERVES 4–6

¾ pound fresh spinach, tough stems removed, thoroughly rinsed and steamed until wilted, about 2 minutes

1½ pounds Goat's Milk Cheese (page 27)

1 egg

½ teaspoon grated nutmeg

1 teaspoon kosher salt

1 cup unseasoned bread crumbs

1½ cups all-purpose flour

½ cup grated Parmesan cheese, plus more for garnish

Rice flour for dusting

6 tablespoons unsalted butter

1. Squeeze the steamed spinach dry. Add the spinach, goat's milk cheese, egg, nutmeg, and salt to the bowl of a food processor fitted with a metal blade and process until smooth. Transfer the spinach mixture to a large mixing bowl. Add the bread crumbs, all-purpose flour, and the ½ cup Parmesan cheese. Stir to fully combine into a dough.

2. Turn the dough out onto a clean, dry, rice flour–dusted work surface. Roll into a log that measures about 10 inches long by 3 inches wide. Cut the log into 4 equal pieces. Use your hands to roll each piece into a 1-inch-diameter rope. You may have to cover your hands with rice flour from time to time to ease the rolling process. Cut each rope into 1-inch pieces.

3. Bring a large pot of salted water (see page 29) to a boil.

4. Add the butter to a 10-inch skillet over high heat and brown, about 2 minutes.

5. Add the gnudi to the boiling water and cook until they float to the top. Cook for 2 more minutes. Use a wire-mesh skimmer to remove the gnudi from the pot and place them directly into the brown butter. Carefully stir to coat the gnudi with the butter.

6. Serve immediately with grated Parmesan cheese.

SWEET POTATO GNOCCHI, olives, capers, tomato, soppressata

THIS SAUCE IS PREPARED *ALLA CACCIATORE*, HUNTER'S STYLE. DISHES MADE IN THIS WAY TRADITIONALLY COULD BE CARRIED WITH YOU WHEN YOU WENT HUNTING. THE INGREDIENTS I USE TEND TO BE CURED OR BRINED ITEMS. I LIKE TO USE SMALL BRINED OLIVES LIKE ALFONSOS, PICHOLINES, OR TAGGIA BECAUSE THEY'RE EASIER TO PIT THAN LARGER OLIVES. TO PIT THEM, YOU SIMPLY PLACE A GROUP OF OLIVES ON A WORK SURFACE, PUT A SMALL HEAVY-BOTTOMED SKILLET OVER THEM, AND PRESS DOWN. THIS SHOULD RELEASE THE PIT ENOUGH SO THAT YOU CAN FINISH THE JOB WITH A FLICK OF YOUR FINGER.

THE OLIVES IN COMBINATION WITH THE EQUALLY BRINY CAPERS, THE ACID-SWEET TOMATOES, AND THE SPICY *soppressata* SALAMI MAKE AN EXTREMELY SAVORY SAUCE THAT'S JUST THE RIGHT COMPANION FOR THE VERY SWEET, SWEET POTATO GNOCCHI.

SERVES 4–6

1 recipe Sweet Potato Gnocchi (page 13)

2 tablespoons unsalted butter

1 clove garlic, thinly sliced

½ pound sliced soppressata, cut into matchsticks

1 cup small pitted brined black olives

¼ cup brined capers, rinsed and drained

1 cup peeled whole San Marzano tomatoes

⅓ cup dry white wine

¼ teaspoon freshly ground black pepper

¼ cup Pasta Water (page 29)

1. Add the butter to a 10-inch skillet over high heat. As soon as the butter has melted, add the garlic, soppressata, olives, and capers. When you see the soppressata start to get crispy, about 3 to 4 minutes, use your hands to squeeze the tomatoes directly into the skillet. Cook for 2 minutes. Stir in the white wine and pepper.

2. Bring a large pot of salted water (see page 29) to a boil. Add the gnocchi to the boiling water and cook until they float to the top. Cook for 1 more minute. Add the ¼ cup pasta water to the skillet. Use a wire-mesh skimmer to remove the gnocchi from the pot and place them directly into the skillet. Carefully stir to combine with the sauce.

3. Serve immediately.

SWEET POTATO GNOCCHI, drunken prunes, amaretti

THIS IS MY VERSION OF THE UNIFICATION OF ITALY. THE PRUNES ARE SOAKED IN DENSE, SWEET MARSALA WINE FROM SICILY IN THE SOUTH, THEN THE WHOLE DISH IS GARNISHED WITH CRUMBLED AMARETTI, THE BITTER ALMOND COOKIES FROM THE NORTHERN REGION OF LOMBARDY.

THESE ARE MODERN GNOCCHI. UNTIL RECENTLY, YOU COULDN'T FIND SWEET POTATOES IN ITALY. BECAUSE I'M SO PARTIAL TO MIXING SWEET AND SAVORY, I WANTED TO FIND ANOTHER WAY TO INCORPORATE SWEET POTATOES INTO MY MENU, CLASSIC ITALIAN INGREDIENT OR NOT.

SERVES 4–6

1 recipe Sweet Potato Gnocchi (page 13)

2 cups coarsely chopped pitted prunes

1 cup dry Marsala

2 tablespoons unsalted butter

½ cup Paster Water (page 29)

6 amaretti cookies (3 double packages), crushed

1. Add the prunes and Marsala to a 10-inch skillet. Turn on the heat to high and bring to a boil. Turn off the heat and remove the skillet.

2. Bring a large pot of salted water (see page 29) to a boil.

3. Add the butter to the prunes. Return the skillet to high heat and melt the butter.

4. Add the gnocchi to the boiling water and cook until they float to the top. Cook for 1 more minute. Add the ½ cup pasta water to the prunes. Use a wire-mesh skimmer to remove the gnocchi from the pot and place them directly into a warm shallow serving platter. Pour the prunes over the top. Garnish with the crushed amaretti.

5. Serve immediately.

BUTTERNUT SQUASH GNOCCHI, sausage, wild mushrooms, almonds

Il Poggio dei Petti Rossi, where Colleen and I worked one summer, is an *AGRITURISMO*, a working farm regulated by the Italian government that offers its guests food produced on the farm or grown locally, and lodging. Il Poggio is situated high on a hill in a lovely, cool setting thick with olive trees, lemon trees, and lentil bushes. In addition to offering accommodations for guests, the farm is a popular venue for wedding receptions.

I remember preparing food for the wedding feasts. Among the things that we made over and over again were stuffed vegetables: zucchini, tomatoes, and mushrooms. The fillings always included sausage and bread. It was then that I finally understood that sausage didn't lose its integrity when it was used as an ingredient rather than on its own. This dish recalls those thousands of stuffed vegetables that Colleen and I made that summer.

SERVES 4–6

1 recipe Butternut Squash Gnocchi (page 14)	1 pound sweet Italian sausage, casings removed	2 tablespoons unsalted butter
½ cup whole almonds	1 pound wild mushrooms, such as hedgehogs, oysters, or shiitakes, wiped clean and trimmed	¼ teaspoon freshly ground black pepper
2 tablespoons grape seed oil		

1. Preheat the oven to 400°F. Place the almonds on a baking sheet with sides. Toast until golden, about 16 to 18 minutes. Remove the almonds from the hot pan to cool. Coarsely chop.

2. Heat the grape seed oil in a 10-inch skillet over high heat. Add the sausage. Use a wooden spoon to break up the sausage while moving it around the pan. Cook until the pink disappears, about 4 minutes. Add the mushrooms and stir to combine. Cook until the moisture is released from the mushrooms and they become tender and brown, about 8 to 10 minutes. Add the butter and let it brown. Add the chopped almonds and pepper. Lower the heat to a simmer.

3. Bring a large pot of salted water (see page 29) to a boil. Add the gnocchi to the boiling water and cook until they float to the top. Cook for 1 more minute. Use a wire-mesh skimmer to remove the gnocchi from the pot and place them directly into the skillet. Carefully stir to combine with the sauce.

4. Serve immediately.

BUTTERNUT SQUASH GNOCCHI,
pistachio pesto

HEN THEY THINK ABOUT PESTO, MOST PEOPLE THINK ABOUT THE POPULAR GREEN SAUCE MADE FROM FRESH BASIL AND SERVED WITH EVERYTHING FROM PASTA TO POACHED SEAFOOD. IN FACT, THE WORD *PESTO* SIMPLY MEANS POUNDED——INGREDIENTS THAT HAVE BEEN SMASHED WITH A PESTLE IN A MORTAR. TODAY, PURISTS LOOK THE OTHER WAY AND USE A BLENDER TO QUICKLY CREATE PESTO.

I PREFER PISTACHIOS OVER ALMOST ANY OTHER NUT. SO IT SEEMED THAT THE VERY GREEN, SUBTLY FLAVORED PISTACHIOS IN COMBINATION WITH THE MORE INTENSELY FLAVORED, BRIGHT ORANGE BUTTERNUT SQUASH GNOCCHI WOULD BE JUST THE RIGHT EXPRESSION OF MY TASTE.

SERVES 4–6

1 recipe Butternut Squash Gnocchi (page 14)	1 cup extra virgin olive oil	2 tablespoons grated Parmesan cheese
1 cup raw shelled pistachio nuts	1 clove garlic	
	1 teaspoon kosher salt	

1. Preheat the oven to 350°F. Place the pistachio nuts on a baking sheet with sides. Toast until you can smell the nuts and they are golden, about 8 to 10 minutes. Let cool.

2. Add the toasted nuts, extra virgin olive oil, garlic, and salt to the jar of a blender and process until coarsely chopped.

3. Bring a large pot of salted water (see page 29) to a boil.

4. Add the pistachio pesto to a 10-inch skillet. Add the Parmesan cheese and stir to combine.

5. Add the gnocchi to the boiling water and cook until they float to the top. Cook for 1 more minute. Use a wire-mesh skimmer to remove the gnocchi from the pot and place them directly into the skillet. Carefully stir into the sauce.

6. Serve immediately.

RICOTTA GNOCCHI, cauliflower, black olives, capers, tomato, pine nuts

I N ANSWER TO CUSTOMER REQUESTS, I THINK ABOUT PUTTING TOGETHER VEGETAR-IAN DISHES ALL THE TIME. FORTUNATELY FOR ME, THERE'S NO OTHER *CUCINA* IN THE WORLD THAT LENDS ITSELF SO EASILY TO VEGETABLE DISHES AS THE ITALIAN KITCHEN. THIS VEGETARIAN DISH IS SIMILAR IN STYLE TO GNOCCHI, SAUSAGE, CAULIFLOWER, MANILA CLAMS, PEPERONCINI (PAGE 146), WITHOUT THE SAUSAGE AND CLAMS, OF COURSE. THE VEGETABLE-ONLY SAUCE MAKES A PERFECT MATCH FOR THE SOFT, MELT-IN-YOUR-MOUTH RICOTTA GNOCCHI.

SERVES 4–6

1 recipe Ricotta Gnocchi (page 15)

½ cup pine nuts

2 tablespoons grape seed oil

1 clove garlic, thinly sliced

3 cups cauliflower florets

½ cup pitted black olives, such as Kalamata

⅓ cup capers, rinsed and drained

½ cup dry white wine

1 cup tomato puree

¼ teaspoon freshly ground black pepper

1. Preheat the oven to 350°F. Place the pine nuts on a baking sheet with sides. Toast until golden, about 5 to 7 minutes. Let cool.

2. Add the grape seed oil and garlic to a 10-inch skillet. Turn on the heat to high. When the garlic is golden around the edges, about 1 minute, add the cauliflower, olives, and capers. Toss together to combine. Cook until the cauliflower just begins to brown. Add the white wine and reduce by half.

3. Bring a large pot of salted water (see page 29) to a boil.

4. Add the tomato puree to the sauce.

5. Add the gnocchi to the boiling water and cook until they float to the top. Cook for 2 more minutes.

6. Add the pine nuts and pepper to the sauce. Use a wire-mesh skimmer to remove the gnocchi from the pot and place them directly into the skillet. Carefully stir to combine with the sauce.

7. Serve immediately.

LEMON RICOTTA GNOCCHI, nantucket bay scallops, raisins, sliced prosciutto

A FEW WINTERS AGO, SOME FRIENDS CAME IN TO THE NANTUCKET RESTAURANT, AND I WANTED TO MAKE A SPECIAL DISH FOR THEM. IT HAPPENED THAT I HAD SOME JUST-SHUCKED LOCAL BAY SCALLOPS IN THE REFRIGERATOR. I SAUTÉED THE SCALLOPS, THEN TOPPED THEM WITH PAPER-THIN SLICES OF PROSCIUTTO, WHICH IMMEDIATELY MELTED OVER THEM—CREATING THE IDEAL MARRIAGE BETWEEN THE SWEET-AS-SUGAR SCALLOPS AND THE SALTY-SWEET PROSCIUTTO.

BEARING IN MIND THE RULE THAT WHEN YOU CREATE PASTA DISHES YOU SHOULD USE INGREDIENTS THAT ARE SIMILAR IN SIZE SO THAT EVERYTHING GETS PICKED UP IN THE SAME FORKFUL, I'VE REINTERPRETED THE SCALLOPS AND PROSCIUTTO DISH OF YEARS AGO AND PAIRED THE INGREDIENTS WITH LEMON RICOTTA GNOCCHI.

SERVES 4–6

1 recipe Ricotta Gnocchi (page 15), made with 2 tablespoons fresh lemon zest added to the dough

1 tablespoon grape seed oil

1 pound Nantucket bay scallops

½ cup golden raisins

¼ teaspoon freshly ground black pepper

¼ cup dry white wine

12 paper-thin slices imported prosciutto

1. Bring a large pot of salted water (see page 29) to a boil.

2. Add the grape seed oil to a 10-inch skillet over high heat. When the oil begins to smoke, add the scallops.

3. Add the gnocchi to the boiling water. Add the raisins, pepper, and white wine to the skillet, but do not turn over the scallops. As soon as the wine reduces by half, turn off the heat. By now the gnocchi should have floated to the top and cooked for 2 minutes. Use a wire-mesh skimmer to remove the gnocchi from the pot and place them directly into the skillet. Carefully stir to combine with the sauce.

4. Top each serving with 2 slices of prosciutto and serve immediately.

GRAINS
rice, polenta, farro

Grain dishes are the cousins of the more traditional pastas made with dough. When I make sauces for these whole grain dishes, I like to call them toppings. Indeed, they sit on top of the dish and sink into the grains rather than being mixed through. The ingredients that go into the toppings very much depend on the distinct flavor of the grain, and on the season.

about my risotto

I like to use water as the liquid for all of the risotto that I make. If you use a stock like chicken or beef, the protein in the stock tends to break down the rice's starch, which in turn cracks the kernel and makes a risotto that's too mushy for my taste.

Another ingredient that I use which differs from the traditional method is grape seed oil. I use it instead of olive oil to sauté the onions and rice. It's the fat of choice in our restaurants' kitchens—its neutral flavor doesn't compete with that of other ingredients.

As you read through my risotto recipes, you'll notice that I treat risotto almost like my pasta recipes in that there are two separate components in each dish. There's the starch—the risotto itself; and the topping—the sauce. However, when I make a risotto, I think about its creation in a slightly different way from that of a pasta dish. With pasta, the sauce needs to adhere to it, but with risotto, I think of the topping as something that can stand on its own and is the surprise in the center of the dish. In fact, that's how I serve my risotto, with the topping added to the center of the cooked rice.

RISOTTO, rabbit, artichoke, mint pesto

HEN THE FIRST LATE-WINTER TO EARLY-SPRING ARTICHOKES ARRIVE, THIS IS THE RISOTTO THAT I MAKE. I LIKE THE WAY THE ALMOST-BITTER ARTICHOKES COMPLEMENT THE INTENSELY FLAVORED RABBIT. THE MINT PESTO ADDS A ZING TO ALL OF IT.

SERVES 4–6

4 tablespoons grape seed oil

One approximately 3-pound rabbit, cut into 3 sections—legs, saddle, and breasts—each section cut into 2 and trimmed of fat

3½ teaspoons kosher salt

¾ teaspoon freshly ground black pepper

6 artichokes, prepared as on page 48, except cut the artichokes in half

1 lemon for the artichokes

1½ cups dry white wine

10 cups water

½ cup pine nuts

½ cup extra virgin olive oil

1 cup packed fresh mint leaves

1 cup finely chopped onions

2 cups carnaroli rice

3 tablespoons unsalted butter

½ cup grated Parmesan cheese

1. Preheat the oven to 400°F. Add 2 tablespoons of the grape seed oil to an ovenproof casserole. Turn on the heat to medium high. Lay the rabbit pieces on a clean, dry work surface. Sprinkle with 1 teaspoon of the salt and ¼ teaspoon of the pepper. Turn over the rabbit pieces and repeat with another teaspoon of the salt and ¼ teaspoon of the pepper. Add to the by-now smoking grape seed oil. Sear on both sides until golden brown, about 3 minutes on each side.

2. Cook the prepared artichokes in their lemon water for 4 minutes. Quarter them and add to the rabbit. Add 1 cup of the white wine and let it reduce by half, about 3 to 4 minutes. Add 4 cups of the water and bring to a boil. Place the casserole in the oven. Cook until the meat is falling-off-the-bone tender and most of the liquid is absorbed, about 1½ hours. Let cool. Carefully—there will be a lot of little bones—shred the meat from the bones directly into the pot.

3. Lower the oven to 350°F. Place the pine nuts on a baking sheet with sides. Toast until golden, about 5 to 7 minutes. Place the pine nuts in the jar of a blender. Add the extra virgin olive oil, 1 teaspoon of the salt, and the mint and process until finely chopped into a pesto.

4. Add the remaining 2 tablespoons grape seed oil and the onions to a 3-quart saucepan. Turn on the heat to medium. Cook, stirring occasionally, until the onions are translucent, about 3 to 4 minutes. (It's important that the onions don't take on color.)

5. Add the rice to the pan and stir into the onions. Let the rice "toast," or dry out—you will see the kernels become opaque—about 1 to 2 minutes. Agitate the pan from time to time to keep the rice from sticking to the bottom. Add the remaining ½ cup white wine and cook until evaporated. Begin to add the remaining water, 2 cups

at a time. Keep stirring in order to release the starch. Continue to agitate the pan. When a wooden spoon dragged through the rice reveals a pathway, add the next 2 cups water. Add the remaining ½ teaspoon salt and ¼ teaspoon pepper.

6. During the addition of the remaining 2 cups water, add the butter and the Parmesan cheese. Continue to stir until a creamy consistency is achieved and the rice kernels are tender but firm.

7. Add the risotto to a warm shallow bowl. Place the braised rabbit and artichokes, with their pan juices, in the center of the risotto and let them sink into the risotto. Drizzle the mint pesto over the top of the rabbit and around the sides of the risotto. Alternatively, make individual plates for each person to be served.

8. Serve immediately.

RISOTTO, spring frutti di bosco: strawberries, morels, asparagus

THERE ARE TWO TIMES OF THE YEAR WHEN I FEEL YOU CAN HONESTLY MAKE THIS DISH WITH *FRUTTI DI BOSCO*, THE FRUIT OF THE WOODS, WHICH GROW WILD IN THE SPRING AND FALL. FOR THIS RECIPE, THE SPRING VERSION—THERE'S A FALL VERSION ON PAGE 172—I USE INGREDIENTS THAT PLAY OFF ONE ANOTHER TO WAKE UP THE PALATE AFTER A LONG WINTER OF EATING ROOT VEGETABLES. THE WOODY EARTHINESS OF THE MUSHROOMS, THE EVER-SO-SLIGHTLY-BITTER ASPARAGUS, AND THE SWEET-TART, JUICY STRAWBERRIES COMBINE TO MAKE AN APPETITE-WHETTING DISH.

SERVES 4–6

2 tablespoons grape seed oil

1 cup finely chopped onions

2 cups carnaroli rice

½ cup dry white wine

6 cups water

2 teaspoons kosher salt

½ teaspoon freshly ground black pepper

6 tablespoons unsalted butter

½ cup grated Parmesan cheese

½ pound spring mushrooms, such as shiitakes or morels, cleaned, trimmed, and medium sliced

¾ pound asparagus, woody parts removed, stems peeled, cut into 1-inch pieces

1 pound strawberries, hulled and halved

1. Add the grape seed oil and onions to a 3-quart saucepan. Turn on the heat to medium. Cook, stirring occasionally, until the onions are translucent, about 3 to 4 minutes. (It's important that the onions don't take on color.)

2. Add the rice to the pan and stir into the onions. Let the rice "toast," or dry out—you will see the kernels become opaque—about 1 to 2 minutes. Agitate the pan from time to time to keep the rice from sticking to the bottom. Add the white wine and cook until evaporated. Begin to add the water, 2 cups at a time. Keep stirring in order to release the starch. Continue to agitate the pan. When a wooden spoon dragged through the rice reveals a pathway, add the next 2 cups water. Add 1 teaspoon of the salt and ¼ teaspoon of the pepper.

3. During the addition of the remaining 2 cups water, add 3 tablespoons of the butter and the Parmesan cheese. Begin to make the topping.

4. Add the remaining 3 tablespoons butter to an 8-inch skillet over medium heat. When the butter has melted, add the mushrooms and asparagus. Cook until tender, about 4 to 5 minutes. Add the strawberries, the remaining 1 teaspoon salt, and

the remaining ¼ teaspoon pepper. Cook until the strawberries release their juices, about 2 to 3 minutes. Remove the pan from the heat. The risotto is cooked when a creamy consistency is achieved and the rice kernels are tender but firm.

5. Add the risotto to a warm shallow bowl. Place the topping in the center and let it sink into the risotto. Alternatively, make individual plates for each person to be served.

6. Serve immediately.

CORN RISOTTO, sausage, blueberries, thyme

I CONSIDER THIS A FLAVORED RISOTTO BECAUSE THE CORN IS COOKED ALONG WITH THE RICE, NOT WITH THE TOPPING. THE IDEA OF USING BLUEBERRIES WITH RISOTTO CAME TO ME ON NANTUCKET, WHERE THERE'S SUCH AN ABUNDANCE OF THE BERRIES GROWING WILD THAT OUR REFRIGERATOR ALWAYS SEEMED TO BE FULL OF THEM. COLLEEN LOVED TO GO BERRY PICKING, AND OUR CUSTOMERS WOULD LEAVE BASKETS OF BERRIES FOR US BY THE KITCHEN DOOR. COLLEEN WOULD USE THEM FOR TARTS, *GELATI*, *SORBETTI*, *PANNA COTTAS*, AND OTHER DESSERTS AND STILL HAVE LEFTOVERS. IT WAS THEN THAT I BEGAN TO CONSIDER ADDING THEIR TART EARTHINESS TO MY SAVORY DISHES.

SERVES 4–6

2 tablespoons grape seed oil	6 cups water	1 pound sweet Italian sausage, casings removed
1 cup finely chopped onions	1 teaspoon kosher salt	Leaves from 5 sprigs fresh thyme
2 cups fresh corn kernels (from about 2 ears)	½ teaspoon freshly ground black pepper	6 ounces fresh blueberries
2 cups carnaroli rice	6 tablespoons unsalted butter	½ cup grated Parmesan cheese
½ cup dry white wine		

1. Add the grape seed oil, onions, and 1 cup of the corn to a 3-quart saucepan. Turn on the heat to medium. Cook, stirring occasionally, until the onions are translucent, about 3 to 4 minutes. (It's important that the onions don't take on color.)

2. Add the rice to the pan and stir into the onions. Let the rice "toast," or dry out— you will see the kernels become opaque—about 1 to 2 minutes. Agitate the pan from time to time to keep the rice from sticking to the bottom. Add the white wine and cook until evaporated. Begin to add the water, 2 cups at a time. Keep stirring in order to release the starch. Continue to agitate the pan. When a wooden spoon dragged through the rice reveals a pathway, add the next 2 cups water. Add ½ teaspoon of the salt and ¼ teaspoon of the pepper.

3. During the addition of the remaining 2 cups water, begin to make the topping: Add 3 tablespoons of the butter to a medium skillet over medium-high heat. When the butter has melted, add the sausage and thyme. Use a wooden spoon to break up the sausage. Turn the heat to high and cook until the pink disappears. Add the remaining ½ teaspoon salt, the remaining ¼ teaspoon pepper, the remaining 1 cup corn, and the blueberries. Cook until the blueberries have burst, about 2 minutes. Stir the remaining 3 tablespoons butter and the Parmesan cheese into the risotto.

Remove the pan from the heat. The risotto is cooked when a creamy consistency is achieved and the rice kernels are tender but firm.

4. Add the risotto to a warm shallow bowl. Place the topping in the center and let it sink into the risotto. Alternatively, make individual plates for each person to be served.

5. Serve immediately.

RISOTTO, corn, lobster, red pepper, zucchini

*W*HILE I WAS ON NANTUCKET, I BEGAN TO THINK ABOUT WHAT OTHER INGREDI-ENTS I COULD ADD TO CORN AND LOBSTER IN ORDER TO MAKE A CHOWDER. NANTUCKET IS FORTUNATE TO HAVE TWO VERY GOOD TRUCK FARMS THAT PRO-VIDE ISLANDERS AND FOOD BUSINESSES WITH AS MUCH FRESH PRODUCE AS WE NEED. THERE ARE ESPECIALLY TASTY VEGETABLES AVAILABLE THROUGHOUT THE SUMMER AND INTO THE FALL—WHEN LOBSTER IS AT ITS BEST. I CHOSE ZUCCHINI AND RED PEP-PER FOR MY CHOWDER, THEN DECIDED THAT WHAT I REALLY WANTED WAS A CORN AND LOBSTER RISOTTO.

SERVES 4–6

2 tablespoons grape seed oil

1 cup finely chopped onions

2 cups carnaroli rice

½ cup dry white wine

6 cups water

1 teaspoon kosher salt

½ teaspoon freshly ground black pepper

6 tablespoons unsalted butter

¼ cup grated Parmesan cheese

1 cup fresh corn kernels (from about 1 ear)

1 medium zucchini, cut into ½-inch cubes

1 red bell pepper, cut into ½ by ½-inch pieces

1 pound lobster cut into ½ by ½-inch pieces

6 large basil leaves, thinly sliced

1. Add the grape seed oil and onions to a 3-quart saucepan. Turn on the heat to medium. Cook, stirring occasionally, until the onions are translucent, about 3 to 4 minutes. (It's important that the onions don't take on color.)

2. Add the rice to the pan and stir into the onions. Let the rice "toast," or dry out—you will see the kernels become opaque—about 1 to 2 minutes. Agitate the pan from time to time to keep the rice from sticking to the bottom. Add the white wine and cook until evaporated. Begin to add the water, 2 cups at a time. Keep stirring in order to release the starch. Continue to agitate the pan. When a wooden spoon dragged through the rice reveals a pathway, add the next 2 cups water. Add ½ tea-spoon of the salt and ¼ teaspoon of the black pepper.

3. During the addition of the remaining 2 cups of water, add 3 tablespoons of the butter and the Parmesan cheese. Begin to make the topping: Add the remaining 3 tablespoons butter, the corn, zucchini, and red peppers to a medium skillet over high heat. When the butter begins to melt, add the remaining ½ teaspoon salt and the remaining ¼ teaspoon black pepper. Lower the heat to medium high. Cook, stirring occasionally, until the zucchini is tender, about 8 minutes. Add the lobster and cook

for 1 more minute. Turn off the heat and add the basil. The risotto is cooked when a creamy consistency is achieved and the rice kernels are tender but firm.

4. Add the risotto to a warm shallow bowl. Place the topping in the center and let it sink into the risotto. Alternatively, make individual plates for each person to be served.

5. Serve immediately.

RISOTTO, fall frutti di bosco: blueberries, raspberries, corn, mushrooms

I KNEW THAT *FRUTTI DI BOSCO* IS A TERM USED TO COLLECTIVELY DESCRIBE THE WILD BERRIES THAT GROW IN THE FOREST. HOWEVER, I LIKE TO INCLUDE OTHER WILD EDIBLES IN MY DEFINITION. DURING OUR FIRST FALL AT SFOGLIA, ON NANTUCKET, ONE OF OUR CUSTOMERS TOLD US THAT HE HAD FOUND WILD PORCINI GROWING IN THE ISLAND'S STATE FOREST. THAT IMMEDIATELY SPARKED MY INTEREST AND MADE ME WANT TO START FORAGING TO SEE WHAT ELSE I COULD FIND UNDER THE FALLEN LEAVES.

ASIDE FROM THE CORN IN THIS RECIPE, THE FRUTTI DI BOSCO CAN BE FOUND GROWING IN THE WILD ON NANTUCKET.

SERVES 4–6

2 tablespoons grape seed oil

1 cup finely chopped onions

2 cups carnaroli rice

½ cup dry white wine

6 cups water

1½ teaspoons kosher salt

½ teaspoon freshly ground black pepper

6 tablespoons unsalted butter

½ cup grated Parmesan cheese

½ pound assorted wild mushrooms, such as chanterelles, oysters, or porcini, cleaned, trimmed, and medium sliced

1 cup corn kernels (from about 1 ear)

1 cup blueberries

1 cup raspberries

1. Add the grape seed oil and onions to a 3-quart saucepan. Turn on the heat to medium. Cook, stirring occasionally, until the onions are translucent, about 3 to 4 minutes. (It's important that the onions don't take on color.)

2. Add the rice to the pan and stir into the onions. Let the rice "toast," or dry out—you will see the kernels become opaque—about 1 to 2 minutes. Agitate the pan from time to time to keep the rice from sticking to the bottom. Add the white wine and cook until evaporated. Begin to add the water, 2 cups at a time. Keep stirring in order to release the starch. Continue to agitate the pan. When a wooden spoon dragged through the rice reveals a pathway, add the next 2 cups water. Add ½ teaspoon of the salt and ¼ teaspoon of the pepper.

3. During the addition of the remaining 2 cups of water, add 3 tablespoons of the butter and the Parmesan cheese. Begin to make the topping: Add the remaining 3 tablespoons butter to an 8-inch skillet over medium heat. When the butter has melted, add the mushrooms and corn. Cook until tender, about 4 to 5 minutes. Add the remaining 1 teaspoon salt and the remaining ¼ teaspoon pepper. Add the

blueberries and raspberries. Cook until the blueberries burst, about 2 minutes. Remove the pan from the heat. The risotto is cooked when a creamy consistency is achieved and the rice kernels are tender but firm.

4. Add the risotto to a warm shallow bowl. Place the topping in the center and let it sink into the risotto. Alternatively, make individual plates for each person to be served.

5. Serve immediately.

CHESTNUT RISOTTO, sausage, raisins, brown butter

THE LONGER CHESTNUTS COOK, THE MORE THEIR NATURAL STARCH COMES OUT, ADD-
ING CREAMINESS TO WHATEVER THEY'RE COMBINED WITH. SINCE, WHEN MAKING A
RISOTTO, THE IDEA IS TO EXTRACT AS MUCH STARCH FROM THE RICE AS POSSIBLE,
COOKING THE CHESTNUTS WITH IT PRODUCES A SUPER, SILKY DISH.

SERVES 4–6

2 tablespoons grape seed oil

1 cup finely chopped onions

1 cup shelled, peeled, coarsely chopped chestnuts (see page 147)

2 cups carnaroli rice

½ cup dry white wine

6 cups water

1½ teaspoons kosher salt

½ teaspoon freshly ground black pepper

6 tablespoons unsalted butter

1 pound sweet Italian sausage, casings removed

6 small fresh sage leaves

½ cup raisins

¼ cup cognac or brandy

¼ cup grated Parmesan cheese

1. Add the grape seed oil, onions, and chestnuts to a 3-quart saucepan. Turn on the heat to medium. Cook, stirring occasionally, until the onions are translucent, about 3 to 4 minutes. (It's important that the onions don't take on color.)

2. Add the rice to the pan and stir into the onions. Let the rice "toast," or dry out— you will see the kernels become opaque—about 1 to 2 minutes. Agitate the pan from time to time to keep the rice from sticking to the bottom. Add the white wine and cook until evaporated. Begin to add the water, 2 cups at a time. Keep stirring in order to release the starch. Continue to agitate the pan. When a wooden spoon dragged through the rice reveals a pathway, add the next 2 cups water. Add ½ teaspoon of the salt and ¼ teaspoon of the pepper.

3. During the addition of the remaining 2 cups water, begin to make the topping: Add 3 tablespoons of the butter to a medium skillet over medium-high heat. When the butter has melted, add the sausage and sage. Use a wooden spoon to break up the sausage. Cook until the pink has disappeared and the sausage starts to brown, about 4 minutes. Add the raisins, cognac, the remaining 1 teaspoon salt, and the remaining ¼ teaspoon pepper. Lower the heat to a simmer. Stir the remaining 3 tablespoons butter and the Parmesan cheese into the risotto. Remove from the heat. The risotto is cooked when a creamy consistency is achieved and the rice kernels are tender but firm.

4. Add the risotto to a warm shallow bowl. Place the topping in the center and let it sink into the risotto. Alternatively, make individual plates for each person to be served.

5. Serve immediately.

LEMON RISOTTO, roasted bone marrow, limoncello

THERE'S ACTUALLY ANOTHER RECIPE IN THIS BOOK THAT INSPIRED THIS ONE: SPAGHETTI AL LIMONE, ALMOND PESTO, GRATED RICOTTA SALATA (PAGE 77). I KNEW THAT THE SHARP, TANGY LEMON FLAVOR WOULD BE A GOOD COMPLEMENT TO CREAMY RICE, SO I TURNED THE SPAGHETTI DISH INTO A RISOTTO. HOWEVER, I FELT THAT THE RICE NEEDED MORE THAN JUST BUTTERFAT TO SMOOTH OUT THE EDGY LEMON TASTE. THE MEATY MARROW HAD THE SUBSTANCE I WAS LOOKING FOR TO FINISH THIS DISH. MARROW HAS A HISTORY WITH RISOTTO. MANY MILANESE COOKS START THEIR RISOTTO BY MELTING MARROW AND USING IT INSTEAD OF OIL TO SAUTÉ THE ONIONS.

SERVES 4–6

4½ pounds marrow bones, cut into eight 3½-inch pieces (have your butcher do this)

2 tablespoons grape seed oil

1 cup finely chopped onions

2 cups carnaroli rice

½ cup fresh lemon juice (from approximately 3 lemons)

6 cups water

1 teaspoon kosher salt

¼ teaspoon freshly ground black pepper

2 tablespoons unsalted butter

½ cup grated Parmesan cheese, plus more for garnish

½ cup Limoncello (page 23)

1 heaping tablespoon finely chopped flat-leaf parsley

½ teaspoon coarse sea salt

1. Preheat the oven to 400°F. Place the marrow bones cut side down on a baking sheet with sides. Bake until the marrow pulls away from the sides of the bone, about 30 minutes. (You may need the assistance of a paring knife to loosen it.) When the bones are cool to the touch, use a demitasse or other small spoon to push the marrow out onto the baking sheet. Reserve 3 tablespoons of the melted pan fat.

2. Add the grape seed oil and onions to a 3-quart saucepan. Turn on the heat to medium. Cook, stirring occasionally, until the onion is translucent, about 3 to 4 minutes. (It's important that the onions don't take on color.)

3. Add the rice to the pan and stir into the onions. Let the rice "toast," or dry out—you will see the kernels become opaque—about 1 to 2 minutes. Agitate the pan from time to time to keep the rice from sticking to the bottom. Add the lemon juice and cook until evaporated. Begin to add the water, 2 cups at a time. Keep stirring in order to release the starch. Continue to agitate the pan. When a wooden spoon dragged through the rice reveals a pathway, add the next 2 cups water. Add the kosher salt, ⅛ teaspoon of the pepper, the butter, and the ½ cup grated Parmesan cheese.

4. When the addition of the remaining 2 cups water has almost absorbed, begin to make the topping: Add the marrow and the reserved pan fat to a small skillet. Turn on the heat to high. When the fat begins to sizzle, add the Limoncello and the remaining ⅛ teaspoon pepper and reduce by half. The risotto is cooked when a creamy consistency is achieved and the rice kernels are tender but firm.

5. Add the risotto to a warm shallow bowl. Break up the marrow and place it and its sauce in the center and let it sink into the risotto. Garnish with the chopped parsley, grated Parmesan cheese, and sea salt. Alternatively, make individual plates for each person to be served.

6. Serve immediately.

RISOTTO, veal cheeks, blood orange, hazelnuts

ISOTTI IN THE NORTHERN REGIONS OF ITALY ARE ALMOST ALWAYS SERVED AS AN ACCOMPANIMENT TO BRAISED MEATS. FOR EXAMPLE, IN LOMBARDY, RISOTTO AND *OSSO BUCO*, BRAISED VEAL SHANKS, ARE INSEPARABLE.

I WAS INSPIRED BY THE CONCEPT OF SERVING BRAISED MEAT WITH RISOTTO. HOWEVER, AT MY RESTAURANTS I OFFER RISOTTO ONLY AS A FIRST COURSE, SO IN THIS CASE THE MEAT COMPONENT SERVES THE OPPOSITE PURPOSE—IT BECOMES THE ACCOMPANIMENT TO THE RISOTTO.

THIS RECIPE IS MY WAY OF HONORING THE GREAT RISOTTI OF NORTHERN ITALY, WHILE GIVING A LITTLE NOD TO THE SOUTH WITH THE ADDITION OF FRAGRANT, TANGY-SWEET BLOOD ORANGES.

SERVES 4–6

½ cup hazelnuts

1 pound veal cheeks, trimmed and cut into 2 by 2-inch pieces

1½ teaspoons kosher salt

¼ teaspoon freshly ground black pepper

3 tablespoons grape seed oil

1 carrot, peeled, cut into 1-inch half-moons

1 rib celery, cut into 1-inch half-moons

1 cup onions, cut into 1-inch pieces, for the veal

1 cup dry white wine

11 cups water

1 cup finely chopped onions for the risotto

2 cups carnaroli rice

4 tablespoons unsalted butter

½ cup grated Parmesan cheese

3 blood oranges, segmented to yield about ¾ cup with the juice

1. Preheat the oven to 350°F. Place the hazelnuts on a baking sheet with sides. Toast until golden, about 12 minutes. Let cool. Coarsely chop in a mortar with a pestle or in a food processor fitted with a metal blade.

2. Add the veal cheeks, 1 teaspoon of the salt, and the pepper to a large mixing bowl. Toss to evenly coat the veal with the seasonings.

3. Heat 1 tablespoon of the grape seed oil in a heavy-bottomed ovenproof casserole over high heat. When it begins to smoke, place the veal cheeks in the oil and sear on all sides. Add the carrot, celery, and onion pieces. Maneuver the veal cheeks so that the vegetables fit in between them. When the vegetables begin to caramelize—after about 5 minutes—add ½ cup of the white wine. Move the vegetables around so that the wine can deglaze the pot and reduce by half, about 2 minutes. Add 5 cups of the water and bring to a boil. Lower the heat to medium. Cook until falling-off-the-bone tender, about 1¼ to 1½ hours. Turn over the cheeks every 20 minutes.

4. **MAKE THE RISOTTO:** Add the remaining 2 tablespoons grape seed oil and the chopped onions to a heavy-bottomed 3-quart saucepan. Turn on the heat to medium. Cook, stirring occasionally, until the onions are translucent, about 3 to 4 minutes. (It's important that the onions don't take on color.)

5. Add the rice to the pan and stir into the onions. Let the rice "toast," or dry out— you will see the kernels become opaque—about 1 to 2 minutes. Agitate the pan from time to time to keep the rice from sticking to the bottom. Add the remaining ½ cup white wine and cook until evaporated. Begin to add the remaining water, 2 cups at a time. Keep stirring in order to release the starch. Continue to agitate the pan. When a wooden spoon dragged through the rice reveals a pathway, add the next 2 cups water. Add the remaining ½ teaspoon salt.

6. When the addition of the remaining 2 cups water has almost absorbed, add the butter and Parmesan cheese. Turn the heat under the veal cheeks to medium and add the blood orange segments and juice to the veal. The risotto is cooked when a creamy consistency is achieved and the rice kernels are tender but firm.

7. Add the risotto to a warm shallow bowl. Place the veal cheeks in the center and let them sink into the risotto. Scatter the chopped hazelnuts over the top. Alternatively, make individual plates for each person to be served.

8. Serve immediately.

RISOTTO ALL'AMARONE, prunes, crushed amaretti

I SAW RED WINE USED TO MAKE RISOTTO FOR THE FIRST TIME WHEN WE WERE WORK-
ING AT LA CROTA, NEAR ALBA. *RISOTTO AL BAROLO* IS A CLASSIC DISH IN WHICH
BAROLO, A FULL-BODIED RED WINE, IS USED INSTEAD OF THE MORE TRADITIONAL
WHITE WINE.

FOR MY DISH, I'VE CHOSEN ANOTHER FULL-BODIED RED WINE, AMARONE, BECAUSE
ITS LUSH, RIPE FLAVOR WORKS SO WELL WITH THE PRUNES AND AMARETTI.

SERVES 4–6

2 tablespoons grape seed oil	6 cups water	½ cup grated Parmesan cheese
1 cup coarsely chopped onions	1 teaspoon kosher salt	1 cup quartered pitted prunes
2 cups carnaroli rice	½ teaspoon freshly ground black pepper	6 amaretti cookies (3 double packages), crushed
1 cup Amarone wine	4 tablespoons unsalted butter	

1. Add the grape seed oil and onions to a 3-quart saucepan. Turn on the heat to medium. Cook, stirring occasionally, until the onions are translucent, about 3 to 4 minutes. (It's important that the onions don't take on color.)

2. Add the rice to the pan and stir into the onions. Let the rice "toast," or dry out—you'll see the kernels become opaque—about 1 to 2 minutes. Agitate the pan from time to time to keep the rice from sticking to the bottom. Add ½ cup of the Amarone and cook until evaporated. Begin to add the water, 2 cups at a time. Keep stirring in order to release the starch. Continue to shake the pan. When a wooden spoon dragged through the rice reveals a pathway, add the next 2 cups water. Add the salt and pepper.

3. During the addition of the remaining 2 cups water, add 3 tablespoons of the butter and the Parmesan cheese. Begin to make the topping: Add the prunes, the remaining ½ cup Amarone, and the remaining 1 tablespoon butter to a small skillet. Turn on the heat to medium high. Reduce the liquid to a syrup, about 8 to 10 minutes.

4. Add the risotto to a warm shallow bowl. Place the topping in the center and let it sink into the risotto. Garnish with the crushed amaretti. Alternatively, make individual plates for each person to be served.

5. Serve immediately.

RISO VENERE, seppie, cipollini, peperoncini

MY FRIEND SUSAN SIMON, WHO HAS LIVED, COOKED, AND SHOPPED FOR FOOD IN ITALY, INTRODUCED ME TO *riso Venere* A FEW YEARS AGO. IT IMMEDIATELY APPEALED TO ALL MY SENSES. I LIKED ITS CHEWY TEXTURE, ITS PLEASING FRAGRANCE, AND THE WAY IT LOOKED. I SEARCHED OUT MORE INFORMATION ABOUT THIS BLACK RICE—WHICH CAME TO ITALY FROM CHINA, WHERE IT WAS CONSIDERED THE RICE OF THE NOBILITY. I DISCOVERED THAT BECAUSE IT IS A WHOLE RICE, IT CONTAINS—AMONG OTHER NUTRIENTS—ABOUT FOUR TIMES AS MUCH IRON AS WHITE RICE.

I'M STILL EXPERIMENTING WITH WAYS TO FEATURE THIS SPECIAL GRAIN. WHEN I PAIR *SEPPIE* WITH THE BLACK RICE, AS I DO HERE, I LIKE THE ILLUSION THAT THE CUTTLEFISH HAVE ADDED THEIR INK TO THE COLOR OF THE DISH.

SERVES 4–6

3 tablespoons grape seed oil

¾ pound cipollini, (flat onions), large ones cut into quarters, small ones cut in half

1½ pounds seppie or calamari, cut into ¼-inch rings, tentacles left intact

½ teaspoon red pepper flakes

1½ teaspoons kosher salt

2 cups dry white wine

8 cups water

½ cup finely chopped onions

2 cups riso Venere (see Resources, page 194)

¼ teaspoon freshly ground black pepper

2 tablespoons unsalted butter

¼ cup grated Parmesan cheese

1. Add 2 tablespoons of the grape seed oil and the cipollini to a 10-inch skillet. Turn on the heat to medium high. Cook, stirring occasionally, until the cipollini show some color, about 4 to 5 minutes. Turn the heat to high. Add the seppie. Sprinkle the red pepper flakes and ½ teaspoon of the salt over everything and toss to combine. Add 1 cup of the white wine and reduce by half. Add 2 cups water and bring to a boil. Lower the heat to a simmer. Cook, stirring occasionally, until the ingredients are butter tender, about 30 to 40 minutes.

2. Add the remaining 1 tablespoon grape seed oil and the chopped onions to a 3-quart saucepan. Turn on the heat to medium. Cook, stirring occasionally, until the onions are translucent, about 3 to 4 minutes. (It's important that the onions don't take on color.)

3. Add the rice to the pan and stir into the onions. Let the rice "toast," or dry out, about 1 to 2 minutes. Agitate the pan from time to time to keep the rice from sticking to the bottom. Add the remaining 1 cup white wine and cook until evaporated.

Begin to add the remaining water, 2 cups at a time. Keep stirring in order to release the starch (which won't be as much as you get with white rice). Continue to agitate the pan. When a wooden spoon dragged through the rice reveals a pathway, add the next 2 cups water. Add the remaining 1 teaspoon salt and the black pepper.

4. During the addition of the remaining 2 cups water, add the butter and Parmesan cheese.

5. Add the riso Venere to a warm shallow bowl. Place the topping in the center and let it sink into the risotto. Alternatively, make individual plates for each person to be served.

6. Serve immediately.

POLENTA, soppressata piccante, poached eggs

P OLENTA IS MADE ALL OVER ITALY, AND MOST COOKS DON'T ADD MUCH MORE THAN SALT AND BUTTER WHEN COOKING IT. I LEARNED TO ADD GARLIC AND RED PEPPER FLAKES TO POLENTA IN ABRUZZI. SINCE I'M SUCH A FIRM BELIEVER THAT EACH COMPONENT OF A DISH SHOULD HAVE ITS OWN FLAVOR, I QUICKLY ADAPTED THE ABRUZZESE STYLE OF MAKING POLENTA, GIVING THIS PART OF THE DISH ITS OWN PERSONALITY. YOU CAN EAT IT BY ITSELF.

THIS RECIPE USES LESS WATER THAN OTHERS, SO THE POLENTA'S CONSISTENCY WILL BE THICKER, ALMOST LIKE CORN BREAD. BY TOPPING THE POLENTA WITH SPICY SOPPRESSATA SALAMI AND POACHED EGGS, THE DISH BECOMES THE RUSTIC ITALIAN BREAKFAST OF MY DREAMS.

SERVES 4–6

6 tablespoons unsalted butter	4 cups water	½ cup grated Parmesan cheese
¼ teaspoon red pepper flakes	2 cups finely ground cornmeal	6 eggs
Six ¼-inch-thick soppressata slices, cut in half, then cut into ¼-inch sticks	1 small clove garlic, thinly sliced	
	1 teaspoon kosher salt	

1. Fill a 10-inch skillet three-quarters full with water and place over low heat.

2. Add 3 tablespoons of the butter, ⅛ teaspoon of the red pepper flakes, and the soppressata to a small skillet or saucepan over high heat. Cook, agitating the pan from time to time, until the butter and soppressata are browned. Turn off the heat.

3. Add the 4 cups water, the cornmeal, garlic, salt, and the remaining ⅛ teaspoon red pepper flakes to a large saucepan. Turn on the heat to medium high. Whisk continuously until fully incorporated and the consistency is smooth and lump free. (At this point you may want to switch to a wooden spoon to continue to stir.) Add the remaining 3 tablespoons butter and the Parmesan cheese. The mixture will be quite thick; persevere and continue to cook until the polenta begins to pull away from the sides of the pan, about 15 minutes.

4. Turn the heat under the skillet to medium low. Poach the eggs in the simmering water.

5. Add equal portions of polenta to individual warm bowls. Sprinkle an equal portion of soppressata and its sauce over each serving. Top each with a poached egg.

6. Serve immediately.

POLENTA, rock shrimp, peperoncini, brown butter

UTTER IS AN ESSENTIAL INGREDIENT IN THE POLENTA-MAKING PROCESS. IT NOT ONLY BRINGS SUMPTUOUS FLAVOR, BUT ALSO GIVES THE DISH THE KIND OF VISUAL SHIMMER THAT I FIND SO APPEALING.

PINK ROCK SHRIMP COOKED IN BROWN BUTTER, SITTING ON TOP OF BRIGHT YELLOW POLENTA, HIGHLIGHTED WITH A SPRINKLE OF DEEP GREEN CHOPPED PARSLEY, MAKES FOR A TASTY AND ATTRACTIVE DISH.

SERVES 4–6

6 cups water

2 cups finely ground cornmeal

1 small clove garlic, thinly sliced

1½ teaspoons kosher salt

¼ teaspoon red pepper flakes

6 tablespoons unsalted butter

¼ cup grated Parmesan cheese

1 pound rock shrimp, rinsed and patted dry

¼ teaspoon freshly ground black pepper

1 heaping tablespoon finely chopped flat-leaf parsley

1. Add the water, cornmeal, garlic, 1 teaspoon of the salt, and ⅛ teaspoon of the red pepper flakes to a large saucepan. Turn on the heat to medium high. Whisk continuously until fully incorporated and the consistency is smooth and lump free. (At this point you may want to switch to a wooden spoon to continue to stir.) Add 3 tablespoons of the butter and the Parmesan cheese. Continue to cook, stirring continuously, until the polenta pulls away from the sides of the pan, about 15 to 18 minutes.

2. Add the remaining 3 tablespoons butter and the remaining ⅛ teaspoon red pepper flakes to a medium skillet over medium-high heat. When the butter is browned, add the rock shrimp and the remaining ½ teaspoon salt and the black pepper. Cook until the shrimps become opaque, about 2 minutes.

3. Add the polenta to a warm shallow bowl and top with the shrimps and their sauce. Garnish with the chopped parsley. Alternatively, make individual bowls for each person to be served.

4. Serve immediately.

POLENTA, braised dandelion, drunken prunes, marsala

THE CONCEPT OF SERVING BRAISED GREENS WITH POLENTA CAME TO ME WHEN COLLEEN AND I WERE WORKING AT IL CIBRÈO IN FLORENCE. THERE, WE OFTEN MADE *FARINATA*, A SOUP WITH THE INTENSELY FLAVORED *CAVOLO NERO*, OR TUSCAN CABBAGE, THAT WAS THICKENED WITH COARSELY GROUND CORNMEAL.

IN THIS DISH I ADD PRUNES DRUNK ON SYRUPY MARSALA, WHICH HELPS TO CALM THE BITTERNESS OF THE DANDELION GREENS.

SERVES 4–6

2 tablespoons grape seed oil

½ cup coarsely chopped onions

1 cup coarsely chopped pitted prunes

1 cup dry Marsala

¾ to 1 pound dandelion or chicory leaves, rinsed and coarsely chopped

10 cups water

2 teaspoons kosher salt

¼ teaspoon freshly ground black pepper

2 cups finely ground cornmeal

1 small clove garlic, thinly sliced

¼ teaspoon red pepper flakes

3 tablespoons unsalted butter

½ cup grated Parmesan cheese

1. Add the grape seed oil and onions to a large skillet. Turn on the heat to medium. Cook until the onions caramelize, about 7 to 8 minutes. Add the prunes and Marsala and reduce the liquid by half. Stir in the dandelion leaves. Turn the heat to high. When the leaves have wilted, about 2 to 3 minutes, add 4 cups of the water, 1 teaspoon of the salt, and ⅛ teaspoon of the black pepper. Reduce the liquid by half, about 20 minutes.

2. Add the remaining 6 cups water, the cornmeal, garlic, red pepper flakes, the remaining 1 teaspoon salt, and the remaining ⅛ teaspoon black pepper to a large saucepan. Turn on the heat to medium high. Whisk continuously until fully incorporated and the consistency is smooth and lump free. (At this point you may want to switch to a wooden spoon to continue to stir.) Add the butter and Parmesan cheese and continue to cook until the polenta pulls away from the sides of the pan, about 15 to 18 minutes.

3. Add the polenta to a warm shallow bowl and top with the greens and prunes sauce. Alternatively, make individual bowls for each person to be served.

4. Serve immediately.

FARRO POLENTA, tuscan cabbage, onions

HERE'S ANOTHER WAY OF INTERPRETING THE *FARINATA* WITH *CAVOLO NERO* THAT I LEARNED TO MAKE IN FLORENCE. THERE'S SOMETHING VERY SATISFYING ABOUT HOW THE STRONGLY STRUCTURED CABBAGE BEHAVES WHEN IT PAIRS WITH THE SOFT BUT GRAINY FARRO POLENTA. I USE *FARRO SPEZIATO*, OR CRACKED FARRO, TO MAKE THE PORRIDGELIKE BASE FOR THIS DISH.

SERVES 4–6

2 tablespoons grape seed oil	½ cup tomato puree	3 teaspoons unsalted butter
1 cup sliced onions	8 cups water	¼ teaspoon freshly ground black pepper
½ teaspoon red pepper flakes	2 teaspoons kosher salt	½ cup grated Parmesan cheese
1 pound Tuscan cabbage, rinsed, stemmed, leaves ripped into medium pieces	2 cups farro *speziato* (cracked farro)	

1. Add the grape seed oil, onions, and red pepper flakes to a 10-inch skillet. Turn on the heat to medium high. Cook until the onions are translucent, about 1 minute. Add the cabbage, tomato puree, 4 cups of the water, and 1 teaspoon of the salt.

2. Add the farro and the remaining 4 cups water to a 3-quart saucepan over high heat. Whisk continuously until the consistency is porridgelike, about 15 to 20 minutes. Add the butter, the remaining 1 teaspoon salt, and the black pepper. Stir continuously until a wooden spoon dragged through the farro reveals a pathway, about 10 minutes. Stir in the Parmesan cheese. Remove the pan from the heat.

3. When the cabbage liquid is reduced by half, about 25 minutes, remove from the heat.

4. Add the farro polenta to a warm shallow bowl. Place the topping over the farro. Alternatively, make individual plates for each person to be served.

5. Serve immediately.

BUTTERNUT SQUASH FARROTTO, sausage

My first experience with farro was in Umbria when Colleen and I spent a summer working at Il Poggio dei Petti Rossi. I noticed that the grain was used there a lot, mostly as part of soups, or, when the grain was *speziato*—cracked—to thicken them. I became curious, so I picked up one of the cookbooks that was part of the kitchen's collection and started to read about the ancient grain. I learned that in addition to being used in its whole grain and cracked forms, it is also ground into flour and used for bread, pastries, and pasta.

This substantial grain is a good complement to autumn and winter ingredients. In preparing it, my method is like the one I use when I make risotto—which, I imagine, is why I call the dish *farrotto*.

SERVES 4–6

One 1¾- to 2-pound butternut squash, wrapped in aluminum foil	½ cup dry white wine	¼ teaspoon dried oregano
3 tablespoons grape seed oil	6 cups water	2 teaspoons kosher salt
1 cup coarsely chopped onions	¾ pound sweet Italian sausage, casings removed	¼ teaspoon freshly ground black pepper
2 cups whole grain farro	6 tablespoons unsalted butter	⅔ cup grated Parmesan cheese

1. Preheat the oven to 400°F. Bake the squash until soft enough that a tester, or the tip of a sharp paring knife, slips easily into its thickest part, about 1½ hours. Let cool. When cool enough to touch, peel the squash and remove the seeds. It should yield about 2 cups of squash.

2. Add 2 tablespoons of the grape seed oil and the onions to a heavy-bottomed 3-quart saucepan. Turn on the heat to medium. Cook, stirring occasionally, until the onions are translucent, about 3 to 4 minutes. (It's important that the onions don't take on color.)

3. Add the farro to the pan. Let it "toast," or dry out, about 1 minute. Agitate the pan from time to time to keep the farro from sticking to the bottom. Add the white wine and cook until evaporated. Begin to add the water, 2 cups at a time. Stir continuously to keep the farro from sticking to the pan. When a wooden spoon dragged through the farro reveals a pathway, add the next 2 cups water.

4. Make the topping while the farro is cooking: Add the remaining 1 tablespoon grape seed oil to a 10-inch skillet over high heat. When the oil is hot, add the sausage. Use a wooden spoon to break it up into smaller pieces so it can thoroughly render its fat. Cook until the pink has disappeared and the sausage starts to brown, about 4 minutes. Add 2 tablespoons of the butter and let it brown. Add the oregano. Turn off the heat.

5. Add the squash to the farro along with the remaining 2 cups water. Incorporate, leaving some chunks. When the farrotto is a few minutes from completion—the sauce is creamy and the grains plump—add the remaining 4 tablespoons butter, the salt, and pepper. When the butter has melted, add the Parmesan cheese. Continue to cook until the Parmesan has melted and become part of the sauce. Farrotto should be a slightly soupy, wet dish.

6. Add the farrotto to a warm shallow bowl. Place the topping in the center and let it sink into the farrotto. Alternatively, make individual plates for each person to be served.

7. Serve immediately.

resources

WWW.CHEFSWAREHOUSE.COM Through this Web site, you can stock up on all the basics: grape seed oil, doppio zero (00) flour, whole wheat flour, nuts, dried fruits, ricotta cheese, anchovies, San Marzano tomatoes, kosher salt, goat's milk, and cornmeal.

WWW.BUONITALIA.COM Buon Italia has a good selection of high-quality imported Italian groceries, including my favorite brand of dry pasta, Setaro. You'll also find fregula, amaretti cookies, balsamic vinegar, extra virgin olive oil, truffles, rices, farro and farro flour, riso Venere, buckwheat flour, bottarga, and mascarpone.

WWW.SALUMERIABIELLESE.COM This New York City institution makes all its own cured meats: guanciale, speck, sausages, prosciutto, and soppressata. They also import Italian prosciutto.

WWW.GUSTIAMO.COM Find high-end Italian products at this site: carnaroli rice, riso Venere, farro speziato, saffron, capers, bottarga, beans, lentils, and chick peas.

WWW.FORMAGGIOKITCHEN.COM Parmesan cheese, pecorino Romano, fontina, mascarpone, smoked mozzarella, mozzarella di bufala, and, in my opinion, awesome ricotta cheese.

WWW.DARTAGNAN.COM Duck, duck eggs, truffles, and wild mushrooms.

WWW.DAIRYCONNECTION.COM All the cultures for making goat's milk cheese.

WWW.PALMBAYIMPORTS.COM This is a wine distributor's site where you'll find a description of my favorite extra virgin olive oil from Sicily, called Planeta. Palm Bay imports will tell you where to buy it locally.

WWW.ALLFRESHSEAFOOD.COM Sea urchin, rock shrimp.

WWW.NANTUCKETSEAFOOD.NET Call Ted Jensen at Nantucket Seafoods at 1-508-325-6345 for bay scallops, lobster, and clams. He'll pack them in ice and ship them to you.

WWW.BOWERYKITCHENS.COM Hand-crank pasta makers, food mills, wire-mesh skimmers (I like the Chinese bamboo-handled ones), 10-inch skillets, baking dishes.

WWW.KITCHENEMPORIUM.COM Hand-crank and electric pasta makers, and cavatelli makers.

WWW.KITCHENAID.COM Stand mixers and pasta-making attachments.

index

Page numbers in *italics* indicate illustrations.